CREATIVE
C LOUR
for cake decorating
20 NEW PROJECTS FROM BESTSELLING AUTHOR

Lindy Smith

D&C
David and Charles

www.stitchcraftcreate.co.uk

Contents

Introduction

From as long ago as I can remember I have been drawn to colour in all its fascinating shades, tones and combinations. Colour is all around us; it creates moods and feelings; it excites and inspires. As a designer, I love experimenting with new colours and colour combinations, so I'm always looking for fresh inspiration. The colours I choose for a design can draw their inspiration from literally anywhere: the iridescent colours of a butterfly's wing, the subtle colours of a delicate flower petal, the experimental colours of a piece of high-fashion clothing, the fabulous rich colours of a plush cosy cushion, the complementary colours of a stunning birthday card – the list is endless.

I love the fact that colours and how they are used go in and out of vogue, which means that there are always new colours and colour combinations to excite and inspire me, and although not all will necessarily look good on cakes, I'll have fun experimenting with them.

Using colour is very natural for me, but I know from my students that many people find colour confusing and difficult. My intention with this book is to give my readers the confidence they need to use colours in unexpected and interesting ways on their cakes. The introductory section explains the basics of colour theory, as this is an excellent starting point for understanding colours and how to combine them. I have then created detailed cake decorating projects where I have found a colour inspiration that appeals to me and used it to select the colours for the cake. For some of the projects I have kept the colour balance very similar to the inspiration but not always; sometimes I have replicated every colour and other times not, in order to demonstrate a few of the different approaches you too can take.

For each project I have also included a colour mixing guide to show you how I have achieved certain colours. There are often a number of options when mixing edible paste colours into sugarpaste, so do experiment with the paste colours you already have before going out and buying more. I have also provided a visual guide to commercial paste colours (see Index of Paste Colours) to assist you when mixing colours.

To gain colour confidence, start with colours that you are drawn to and feel comfortable using and then begin to experiment away from these. Look closely at the world around you and be open and receptive to new ways of using colour. I find it very rewarding when I create a cake using colours that are not in my natural colour palette – yes, they are harder to work with, yet the result is often no less striking. Remember that colours are very personal, but if you are confident with the colours you are using, others are sure to love them too. Be brave, be bold and don't be afraid to experiment.

As always I'd love to see your creations, so do share them via the Lindy's Cakes Facebook page. To see more of how I use colour on cakes, please visit my website where there is a wealth of cakes and cookie examples just waiting for you to discover. Click on the galleries, the blog and the shop to see cakes in all shapes, sizes and colours.

I hope you find this book an inspiration and that it helps you make new and exciting colour discoveries of your own.

Lindy

www.lindyscakes.co.uk

5

COLOUR
a world of choice

Colour is probably the single most important aspect of decorating a cake, and in my opinion, getting it right is well worth taking time over. Colours are more than just decorations – they create a whole mood and are very powerful. So a little understanding about the science of colour can help you turn a decorated cake into a stunning centrepiece.

Choosing colours

There may be no right or wrong colour combinations, but I know that many people struggle when they have to choose colours for their cakes. The colour wheel, which was originally developed by Isaac Newton in the 17th century, is an excellent tool for visualizing colour relationships. The wheel consists of the colours of the spectrum presented in a circle, and it can be used to identify and apply colour relationships and harmonies in order to create an infinite number of pleasing colour combinations. Colour can be used to dazzle, soothe, charm or excite, all entirely through the choice of specific relationships.

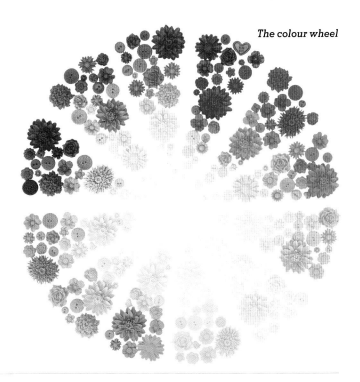

The colour wheel

Five example colour harmony schemes

Colour theory has a set of guiding principles, based on the colour wheel, that helps simplify the task of choosing colours, making it much easier to create harmonious colour combinations. Here are five examples:

MONOCHROMATIC

Using tints, tones and shades from just one colour, this colour scheme is easy to apply due to its simplicity and can be very effective, soothing and authoritative.

ANALOGOUS OR ADJACENT

Using colours lying next to each other on a colour wheel, these easy-to-create schemes are often found in nature and because of their unity and consistency are pleasing to the eye.

COMPLEMENTARY

Using colours that lie opposite on the colour wheel, these colour schemes have a more energetic feel, as the high contrast between the colours creates a vibrant look.

TRIADIC

Using three colours equidistantly spaced on the wheel, these schemes are some of the least recognizable. They are vibrant but comfortable to the eye.

POLYCHROMATIC

Using any five or more colours on the colour wheel.

"All colours are friends with their neighbours and the lovers of their opposites" – Marc Chagall

Three example colours; twelve colour schemes

Here I have taken three example colours – orange, blue and pink – and illustrated four colour harmony scheme options for each.

monochromatic schemes

analogous schemes

triadic schemes

complementary schemes

Other colour considerations

Context

The context of a colour or colours is very important, as one colour will affect another. I have shown examples of this at the end of several of the cake projects by using different background colours to display my cupcakes and cookies. The results can be quite striking.

Composition

Differing ratios of colours also have a large impact on how each colour is perceived,

and again I have created examples to demonstrate this phenomenon at the end of some of the projects.

Colour temperature

Warm colours – oranges and reds – are vivid and energetic colours, while cool blues and greens are soothing, giving the impression of calm. It has been proven that we literally feel colour temperature, with red making our pulses race and blues slowing our heart rates. There are cooler and

warmer versions of every colour; for example, red mixed with larger amounts of blue is a cooler colour than a red-orange. When placed against a cool colour, a warm colour will appear more intense than if placed against another warm or neutral colour.

Personal view

Interestingly, we all see colours slightly differently and this changes as we age.

Mixing colours

Today we are spoiled, as sugarpaste (rolled fondant) is available in an ever-increasing array of colours. However, to just use these is limiting, so I think it is important to master the skills of colour mixing. Again, the colour wheel is a useful tool to help us.

Colour wheel mixes

A 12-segment wheel consists of the following:

◊ Three primary (unmixable) colours – red, blue and yellow – equally spaced around the circle

◊ Three secondary colours – mixtures of two of the primary colours in equal quantities

◊ Six tertiary colours – made by mixing primary and secondary colours together

primary colours

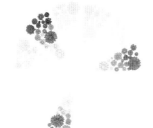

secondary colours

tertiary colours

"In order to use colour effectively it is necessary to recognize that colour deceives continually" – Josef Albers

Here is an example that simplifies the mixing process still further. The colours that are essential to have – the primaries – are shown as large hearts; the secondary colours, mixed from the primaries, as small hearts; and the brown flower in the middle shows what happens when the opposite colours in the circle are mixed.

The theory states that there are three primary colours from which all other colours can be made, but when you start mixing your own sugarpaste colours you will find that, although the primaries should produce all the other colours, the reality doesn't quite match up to the theory.

Tints, shades and tones

Changing colours to create the perfect blend is important when mixing colours for cakes, so it helps to understand how tints, shades and tones of a certain colour can be created. Basically, this is how it works:

◊ If a colour is made lighter by adding white, the result is called a **tint.**
◊ If black is added to a colour, the darker version is called a **shade.**
◊ If grey is added to a colour, it is called a **tone.**

For my example colour palette, I have taken the two primary colours of yellow and red and then mixed them together to create the secondary orange and two tertiary colours. On the left-hand side I have demonstrated a range of tints where white has been added to the colours to lighten them, and on the right-hand side, firstly a row of tones where grey has been added and then a single example of a shade where black has been mixed in. Note what happens once black has been added, particularly to the orange and yellows.

Knowing that this colour change happens comes with experience and experimentation, so why not have a go at mixing your own examples, starting with just two colours – you never know what wonderful colours you will discover.

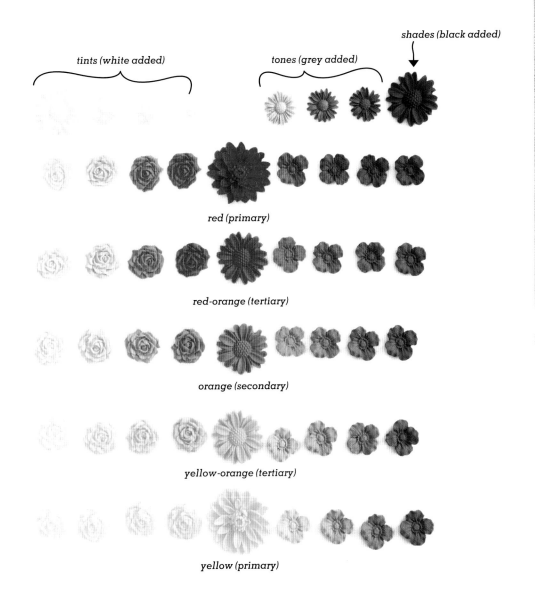

tints (white added)

tones (grey added)

shades (black added)

red (primary)

red-orange (tertiary)

orange (secondary)

yellow-orange (tertiary)

yellow (primary)

… colour – a world of choice

Colouring sugarpaste

Colouring sugarpaste can be a very sticky and messy process, so before you begin, rub your hands with white vegetable fat (shortening) to help prevent your skin taking on the paste colour, and have a bar of old-fashioned soap to hand with which to wash your hands clean afterwards.

A

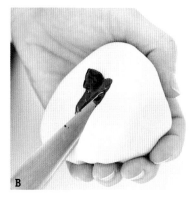

B

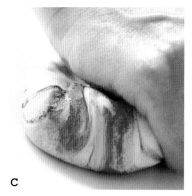

C

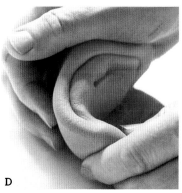

D

1 If you only want to colour a small amount of paste or you wish to make a pastel colour, place a little paste colour, not liquid colour, on the end of a cocktail stick (toothpick) and add it to your sugarpaste (**Fig A**). Then knead the colour into the paste.

2 If you wish to create a deep rich colour, add a larger amount of paste colour to the end of a palette knife and add to the paste (**Fig B**).

Knead the paste to distribute the colour; initially the paste will look streaky (**Fig C**), but as you continue to knead the colour will become uniform (**Fig D**). Add more paste colour as necessary to achieve a deeper colour. If the sugarpaste becomes really sticky due to the amount of paste colour used, add a pinch of gum tragacanth or CMC to firm it up a little and leave to rest.

tip STORE YOUR COLOURED SUGARPASTE IN A PLASTIC BAG IN AN AIRTIGHT CONTAINER.

Changing a mixed colour

1 If you wish to change the colour of the mixed sugarpaste, it is much easier to add another coloured sugarpaste rather than to add another paste colour (**Fig A**). You will find it easier to monitor how much colour to add and you will feel more in control.

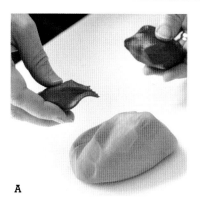

A

Colouring larger quantities

1 If you wish to colour large amounts of sugarpaste, it is easier to colour a smaller amount of sugarpaste a shade darker than you require and then gradually add this into a larger amount, rather than trying to colour the paste all in one go (**Fig A**).

2 Once you are happy with your chosen colour (**Fig B**), pop it into an airtight plastic bag and put to one side until ready to use.

A   **B**

Colour variables

Some variable factors can affect the colours that you mix, including the following:

Time Colours often darken over time, so if possible leave your paste to rest for a few hours before using – this way, you won't have to add so much colour.

Ingredients White vegetable fat (shortening), margarine and butter all make colours turn darker, whereas lemon juice softens colours.

Light Some colours, especially pinks, purple and blues, do fade in bright light, so protect your paste and finished creations from direct sunlight or bright lights.

Useful mixing tips

Allow time Don't underestimate how long it takes to mix colours that blend and harmonize.

Work in daylight Always try to use daylight to select and mix your colours to give the most accurate results.

Start with sugarpaste It is much easier to mix colours into sugarpaste than modelling paste, so mix the colour you require first before adding gum tragacanth to make modelling paste.

Add dark to light It only takes a little of a dark colour to change a light colour, but it takes much more of a light colour to change a dark colour.

Use single pigments For the brightest, most intense colours, use those made from one pigment only, e.g. Squires Kitchen's daffodil (yellow) and Sugarflair's ice blue, so check the label of your paste colours to see how many pigments the paste contains.

Use tints, not white A tint may look white when placed with other colours on your cake, but it will be much more pleasing on the eye than a stark true white.

Blending colours One trick I often use is to add a little of one colour to another to change it fractionally so that the two colours are more in harmony with one another. You will see examples of this in the colour mixing guides for the main cake projects.

Index of paste colours

Here I have taken three of the major brands currently available in the UK – Squires Kitchen, Sugarflair and Wilton (EU) – and shown the colours and tints that can be created using them to provide a visual reference. This colour index has been compiled to help you get to know your colours and to show that colours made with the same edible pigment can vary dramatically in appearance. I hope you find it useful.

Note

The only truly accurate colours are ones mixed by hand using edible colours. This book is printed with ink and produced as an ebook to be viewed on screen, so there will be variations between the colours shown in print and on screen, and the actual colours achievable.

Colour	E numbers
Squires Kitchen	
berberis (light orange)	E104, E129
blackberry	E129, E133, E104
bluebell (navy blue)	E133, E151
bluegrass	E133, E104
bordeaux	E151, E129
bulrush (dark brown)	E104, E129, E133
cactus	E133, E104
chestnut (flesh)	E104, E129, E133
cyclamen (ruby)	E129, E151
daffodil (yellow)	E104
dark forest	E104, E133, E129
desert storm	E104, E129, E133
fern	E133, E104
fuchsia	E122, E129
gentian (ice blue)	E133
holly/ivy (dark green)	E104, E129, E133
hyacinth	E133, E151
hydrangea	E133, E104
jet black	E153
leaf green	E104, E129, E133
lilac	E129, E151
marigold (tangerine)	E104, E129
mint (Xmas green)	E133, E104
nasturtium (peach)	E104, E129
olive	E104, E133, E129
plum	E151, E129
poinsettia (Xmas red)	E129
poppy	E129, E104
rose	E122
sunflower	E104, E129
sunny lime	E104, E129, E133
teddy bear brown	E104, E129, E133
terracotta	E129, E104, E133
thrift	E129, E151
vine	E133, E104
violet (purple)	E129, E151
wisteria	E151, E133

Sugarflair	
autumn leaf	E102, E155
bitter lemon/lime	E102, E133
black extra	E124, E133, E104
caramel/ivory	E102, E155, E133
chestnut	E155
Christmas green	E104, E155, E133
Christmas red	E124, E129
claret	E122, E133
cream	E172, E104
dark brown	E155, E133
dusky pink/wine	E129, E122, E133
egg yellow/cream	E104, E110
eucalyptus	E133, E155, E122, E104
foliage green extra	E102, E133, E155
gooseberry	E102, E155, E133
grape violet	E122, E133
holly green	E133, E155, E102
ice blue	E133
liquorice	E153
melon	E102
mint green	E102, E133
navy	E133, E122, E155
paprika/flesh	E110, E129, E155
party green	E104, E133
peach	E110, E124
pink	E129, E122,
red extra	E124, E129
ruby	E122, E129
spruce green	E155, E102, E133
tangerine/apricot	E110, E129

Wilton	
black	E129, E133, E102
golden yellow	E102, E110
ivory	E110, E102
leaf green	E102, E133
pink	E122, E102
red-red	E129
royal blue	E133, E122
violet (purple)	E122, E133

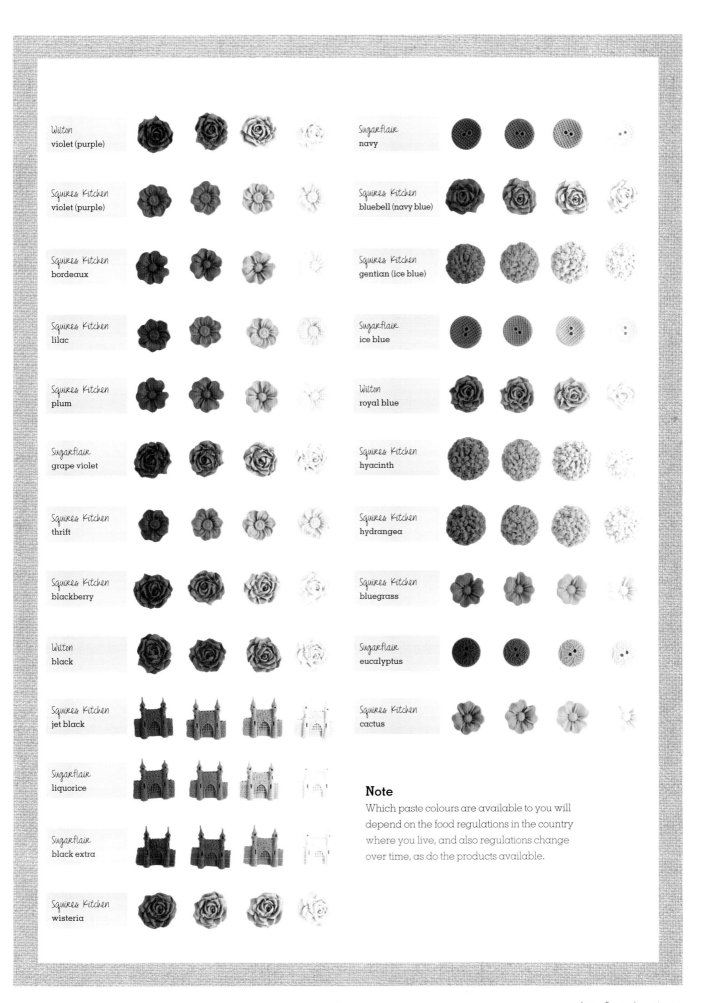

Wilton
violet (purple)

Squires Kitchen
violet (purple)

Squires Kitchen
bordeaux

Squires Kitchen
lilac

Squires Kitchen
plum

Sugarflair
grape violet

Squires Kitchen
thrift

Squires Kitchen
blackberry

Wilton
black

Squires Kitchen
jet black

Sugarflair
liquorice

Sugarflair
black extra

Squires Kitchen
wisteria

Sugarflair
navy

Squires Kitchen
bluebell (navy blue)

Squires Kitchen
gentian (ice blue)

Sugarflair
ice blue

Wilton
royal blue

Squires Kitchen
hyacinth

Squires Kitchen
hydrangea

Squires Kitchen
bluegrass

Sugarflair
eucalyptus

Squires Kitchen
cactus

Note

Which paste colours are available to you will
depend on the food regulations in the country
where you live, and also regulations change
over time, as do the products available.

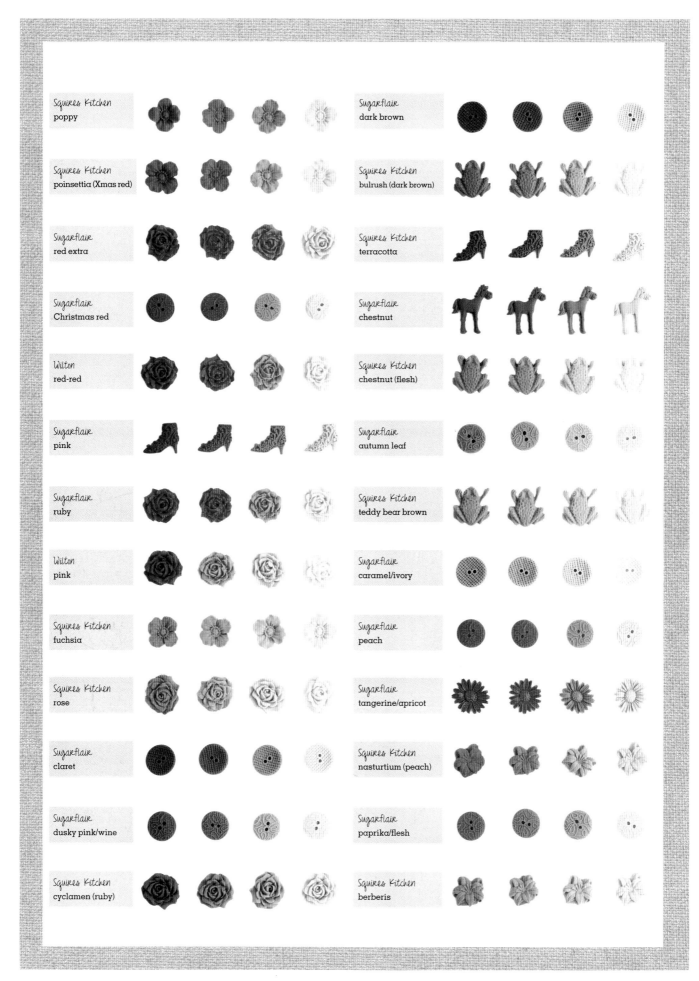

Squires Kitchen poppy					Sugarflair dark brown				
Squires Kitchen poinsettia (Xmas red)					Squires Kitchen bulrush (dark brown)				
Sugarflair red extra					Squires Kitchen terracotta				
Sugarflair Christmas red					Sugarflair chestnut				
Wilton red-red					Squires Kitchen chestnut (flesh)				
Sugarflair pink					Sugarflair autumn leaf				
Sugarflair ruby					Squires Kitchen teddy bear brown				
Wilton pink					Sugarflair caramel/ivory				
Squires Kitchen fuchsia					Sugarflair peach				
Squires Kitchen rose					Sugarflair tangerine/apricot				
Sugarflair claret					Squires Kitchen nasturtium (peach)				
Sugarflair dusky pink/wine					Sugarflair paprika/flesh				
Squires Kitchen cyclamen (ruby)					Squires Kitchen berberis				

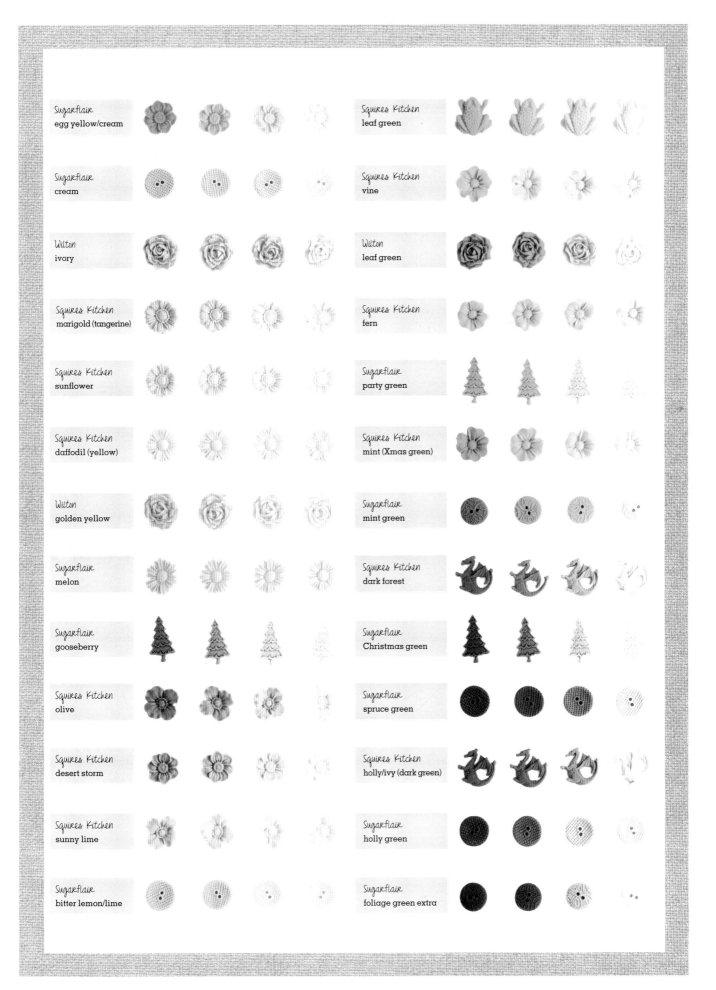

Sugarflair egg yellow/cream					Squires Kitchen leaf green			
Sugarflair cream					Squires Kitchen vine			
Wilton ivory					Wilton leaf green			
Squires Kitchen marigold (tangerine)					Squires Kitchen fern			
Squires Kitchen sunflower					Sugarflair party green			
Squires Kitchen daffodil (yellow)					Squires Kitchen mint (Xmas green)			
Wilton golden yellow					Sugarflair mint green			
Sugarflair melon					Squires Kitchen dark forest			
Sugarflair gooseberry					Sugarflair Christmas green			
Squires Kitchen olive					Sugarflair spruce green			
Squires Kitchen desert storm					Squires Kitchen holly/ivy (dark green)			
Squires Kitchen sunny lime					Sugarflair holly green			
Sugarflair bitter lemon/lime					Sugarflair foliage green extra			

15

... index of paste colours

CAFÉ COUTURE

Colour inspiration...

There is nothing I like more than visiting a coffee shop, relaxing in a comfy chair and sipping a really smooth cappuccino. It was on one such occasion that I happened to notice the shop's colour scheme and realized that it would also work very well on a cake. I always carry a camera with me for such occasions, so a few snaps and one coffee later I had the beginnings of a plan. Although the photo doesn't show the staff, they were wearing bright pink uniforms, which really made the setting much more vibrant. I made a mental note to include this colour as well.

COLOUR-BRANDED COFFEE SHOP; INTERESTINGLY, OTHER BRANCHES IN THE CHAIN USE THE BRAND COLOURS IN VARYING PROPORTIONS.

SPLIT COMPLEMENTARY COLOUR SCHEME

This is a variation on the standard complementary scheme, which uses a colour and the two colours adjacent to its complementary. This provides high contrast without the strong tension of the complementary scheme.

A DEEP PURPLE BRAMBLE LEAF AGAINST COMPLEMENTARY LIME GREEN MOSS.

THIS PINK ZINNIA PERFECTLY COMPLEMENTS THE GREEN LEAVES OF ITS BACKGROUND.

"Colour is a means of exerting a direct influence on the soul" – Wassily Kandinsky

A NEUTRAL CREAM ALLOWS THE FLORA TO DOMINATE IN THIS TIFFANY-STYLE LAMPSHADE.

A DELICATE SEDUM FLOWER HEAD DISPLAYING A STRIKING MIX OF PINKS.

split complementary colour scheme ...

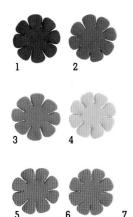

Mixing the colours

To recreate the colours I have used, add the following paste colours to white sugarpaste (rolled fondant) or use the sugarpaste I have suggested:

1 dark brown: dark brown (SF) and chestnut (SF)

2 dark berry purple: M&B amethyst plus thrift (SK) and rose (SK)

3 dark green: mint (SK) and gooseberry (SF)

4 lime green: vine (SK) and gooseberry (SF) plus a touch of autumn leaf (SF) and dark green as mixed above

5 dark pink: rose (SK)

6 berry pink/coral: M&B pink sugarpaste plus red extra (SF) and a touch of rose (SK)

7 ivory: ivory sugarpaste or white sugarpaste plus a touch of autumn leaf (SF) and chestnut (SF)

You will need

materials

cakes: 3 round cakes 23cm (9in), 18cm (7in) and 12.5cm (5in), all 7.5cm (3in) high

sugarpaste (rolled fondant): 1.2kg (2lb 10oz) dark berry purple; 700g (1lb 9oz) berry pink/coral; 900g (2lb) dark brown; 600g (1lb 5oz) ivory

modelling paste: 100g (3½oz) each dark berry purple, berry pink/coral and ivory; 50g (2oz) each dark pink, dark brown, lime green and dark green

buttercream

royal icing, for stacking cakes

white vegetable fat (shortening)

sugar glue

equipment

cake boards: 2 round drums 20cm (8in) or less to act as temporary spacers; 2 round petal drums 30cm (12in) and 25.5cm (10in); 3 round hardboards 18cm (7in), 12.5cm (5in) and 7.5cm (3in)

6 dowels

perfect pearls 10mm (⅜in), 8mm (⁵⁄₁₆in) and 6mm (¼in) mould BR129 (FI)

cutters: five-petal large blossom F6B (OP); five-petal rose (FMM); 3.5cm (1⅜in) pointed oval (LC); 5cm (2in) five-petal (PME); 3cm (1¼in) eight-petal flower from flat floral sugarcraft cutter collection – set 1 (LC); 17mm (⅝in) wide daisy centre stamp (JEM); clematis leaves part of clematis and leaves set (PC)

2 small pieces of non-slip matting

waxed paper

tip I HAVE USED A RANGE OF FLOWER CUTTERS FROM MY TOOLBOX THAT WORK WITH ONE ANOTHER, BUT I SUGGEST YOU EXPERIMENT WITH THE CUTTERS YOU HAVE YOURSELF TO SEE HOW THEY WORK TOGETHER

... café couture

Preparation

1 Place one small piece of non-slip matting on top of one of the small round cake drums, then position the largest petal drum on top. This allows the board edges to be covered more easily with sugarpaste and means that the board is more movable.

2 Dip a paintbrush into cooled boiled water and use it to dampen the edges of the petal drum.

3 Roll out 850g (1lb 14oz) of the dark berry purple sugarpaste between 5mm (⅛in) spacers, using white vegetable fat to prevent sticking.

Lift up the paste, using a rolling pin for support, and place it over the board. Using a smoother, smooth the paste with a circular motion to give a level surface, then use the palm of your hand to smooth the curved edge. Trim the sugarpaste flush with the underside of the board, taking care to keep the cut horizontal (**Fig A**). Set aside to dry.

4 Repeat using the smaller petal cake drum and the berry pink/coral sugarpaste.

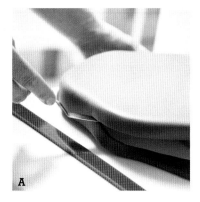

A

Stage one

Carving the cakes

1 Level each of the cakes (see Levelling Cakes).

2 Turn the base cake over so that it rests on its levelled top. Place the 18cm (7in) round hardboard or disc of waxed paper in the centre of the base cake. Using a knife, make a shallow cut around the board or disc to mark its position so that if it slips it is easier to replace.

3 Carve from the edge of the board down to the outside edge of the cake – the surface that is resting on your work surface. Use small cuts to ensure that you don't carve away too much cake (**Fig A**).

4 Turn the cake back over and straighten the cut of the sides if necessary. Also check that the cake is symmetrical and adjust as required. Use scissors or a small knife to carefully curve the top edge to give a rounded appearance.

5 Repeat for the smaller cakes, using the 12.5cm (5in) hardboard for the 18cm (7in) cake and the 7.5cm (3in) one for the 12.5cm (5in) cake.

A

tip WHEN CARVING A SHAPE FROM CAKE, ALWAYS STEP BACKWARDS TO CHECK YOUR PROGRESS AND GET AN OVERALL VIEW.

Covering the cakes

1 Stick the 23cm (9in) cake onto the 18cm (7in) hardboard using buttercream, then place on waxed paper and cover the whole cake in a thin layer of buttercream with a palette knife.

2 Roll out the dark brown sugarpaste and use to cover the cake. Carefully ease in the fullness of paste around the side of the cake – start near the top of the side and use a cupped hand to stroke the paste in an upwards direction, gradually lowering your hand down the side until all the paste is eased in. Be careful, as you don't want any pleats; if one starts to form, pick the paste up around the pleat to redistribute it and try again.

3 Smooth the sugarpaste, firstly using a smoother to iron out any irregularities in the surface and then the base of your hand to smooth and polish the top edge. While pressing down, run the flat edge of the smoother around the cake base to create a cutting line. Cut away the excess paste with a palette knife.

4 Repeat for the remaining tiers, placing the cakes individually on waxed paper with the respective cake boards underneath each cake, before covering with the appropriate coloured sugarpaste. Set aside to dry.

Assembling the cakes

Stick the two covered boards together with royal icing, positioning the petals as shown in the main photo. Dowel the two larger cakes and stack all the cakes centrally on the covered boards (see Dowelling/Stacking Cakes).

Stage two

Adding the beading

1 To create the purple beading for the middle tier, knead some dark berry purple modelling paste to warm and roll into a long sausage about 1.2cm (½in) thick. Place on top of the 10mm (⅜in) section of the perfect pearls mould and press down firmly with firstly your fingers and then the back of a Dresden tool. Use a palette knife to cut away the excess paste (**Fig A**), then release the pearls by flexing the mould along its length so that the pearls fall out without breaking or distorting (**Fig B**). Repeat

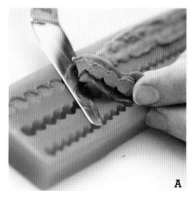

A

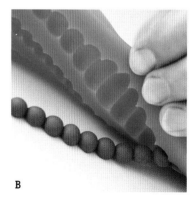

B

until you have created enough pearls to go around the base of the middle tier. Allow the pearls to firm up a little before attaching them in position on the cake using sugar glue.

2 Repeat to make 8mm (⁵⁄₁₆in) berry pink/coral pearls for the top tier, 8mm (⁵⁄₁₆in) ivory pearls for the base and 6mm (¼in) brown pearls for the petal cake board.

... café couture

Creating the flowers

A

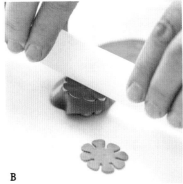

B

C

1 Thinly roll out the berry pink/coral, dark berry purple and dark pink modelling pastes using 1mm (¹⁄₃₂in) spacers. Use the largest five-petal blossom cutter to cut out two flowers from each colour (**Fig A**).

2 To add shape to the flower, place it centrally into a former – ready-made polystyrene formers are available but you can easily make your own using foil cupped over a round pastry cutter, cup or glass. Gently pinch the tip of each petal to give some movement and variation to the petals.

3 Thinly roll out berry pink/coral, dark brown and ivory modelling pastes and use the five-petal rose cutter to cut one flower from each colour. Place in a former and pinch each petal as before.

4 Referring to the main cake for colour suggestions, cut five petals for each flower using the pointed oval cutter and three smaller five-petal flowers, placing the smaller flowers in formers to help give them shape.

5 Cut out three eight-petal flowers using the metal double-sided cutter. To achieve a clean cut, rather than pressing the cutter into the modelling paste, place the paste over the cutter and roll over it with a rolling pin (**Fig B**). Run your finger over the edges of the cutter, turn the cutter over and carefully press out the paste with a soft paintbrush. Place in a small cupped former.

6 For the flower centres, press a ball of modelling paste firmly into the daisy centre stamp; use just enough to fill the mould without spilling out over the edges (**Fig C**). The moulded paste should come away cleanly from the mould attached to your thumb.

7 Allow all the flowers in the formers to partially dry; how long this takes depends on atmospheric conditions. If it's very dry, your paste will firm up quickly; if it's very humid, you may need to reduce the humidity to allow the icing to start to set.

Creating the leaves

1 Separately warm and thinly roll out the two green modelling pastes. Leave your rolled-out paste for a moment or two and then cut out a selection of leaves using the clematis leaf cutter (**Fig A**).

2 Take a few sheets of kitchen paper (paper towel) and scrunch up small pieces to act as formers for your leaves. Place the cut-out leaves over the paper shapes to add curl and movement (**Fig B**). You may also wish to pinch together the base of some of the leaves for extra shape. Allow the leaves to partially dry.

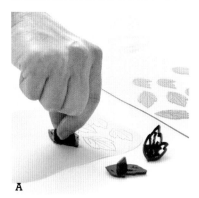

A

B

A

B

C

Assembling the flowers

1 Once the petals of the flowers retain their shape but still have a little flexibility, start to build the layered flowers on a flat surface. Position the flowers, petals and daisy centre as shown, sticking each layer in place with sugar glue (**Fig A**). Now that the petals are no longer constrained by a former, you will find that they fall back towards the flat surface and create a much more open-formed flower.

2 Once the three flowers are complete, attach to the cake with sugar glue, referring to the finished cake for placement. Add the partially dried leaves to either side of each flower as shown.

3 The flowers and leaves should still have some flexibility at this stage, so make any adjustments you wish, such as re-pinching the flower petals (**Fig B**). Finally, create

additional space between the petals of the flower and between the leaves by adding small amounts of twisted kitchen paper (**Fig C**). Leave to dry.

4 Remove all paper from the cake before serving.

... café couture

You will need

platform stiletto cookies and cutter (LC)

70g (2½oz) sugarpaste (rolled fondant) per cookie, colours as for the main cake

modelling paste, colours as for the main cake

cutters: clematis leaves part of clematis and leaves set (PC); 3.5cm (1⅜in) and 3cm (1¼in) five-petal (PME); daisy marguerite (PME); small five-petal flower from fantasy flower set (PC); small daisy centre stamp (JEM)

piping gel

Well-heeled cookies

For this alternative project I have chosen to use the pretty berry pink for the main body of the shoe and decorate it with a similar flower to the main cake using the cake's colour palette. However, how attractive or appealing the cookie looks once complete is very dependent on the background colour on which it is displayed. The backgrounds all complement the decoration, but they affect the colours used differently. When placed on the green background, for example, it enhances the colours of the leaves, so these become quite noticeable.

1 Separately roll out some brown and berry pink/coral sugarpaste to a thickness of 5mm (⅕in), ideally using spacers. Cut out a shoe shape from each colour using the cookie cutter. Then use a knife to separate the shoe tops from the heels.

2 Paint piping gel over the cookie to act as a glue.

3 Using a clean palette knife and a quick swiping action so as not to distort the shape, position the palette knife under the berry pink sugarpaste shoe top before carefully lifting it and placing on top of the cookie. Add the brown sugarpaste heel, making sure that the two paste shapes abut neatly.

4 Use a cutting wheel to mark the heel and sole of the shoe.

5 Use the tip of one of the leaf cutters to emboss a pattern around the upper edge of the shoe.

6 Create the flower and leaves as for the main cake but using the suggested cutters so that the scale is more appropriate.

WHEN PLACED ON THE PINK BACKGROUND, THE PINKS OF THE SHOE BLEND INTO THE BACKGROUND SO THAT THE IVORY PETALS AND BROWN FLOWER CENTRE ARE MORE DOMINANT. THE SAME HAPPENS TO THE PURPLE PETALS ON THE PURPLE BACKGROUND, MAKING THE PINK ONES MORE PROMINENT. IT IS ONLY ON THE NEUTRAL BROWN BACKGROUND THAT ALL THE ELEMENTS OF THE DECORATED COOKIE ARE CLEARLY SEEN.

"Any colour works if you push it to the extreme" – Massimo Vignelli

... café couture

CREATIVE
CLOCK TOWER

Colour inspiration...

Inspired by the ancient city of Rome, I have selected the colours for this cake from a photograph I took looking down a narrow cobbled street in the old Jewish ghetto area of the city. Not far from the busy historic heart of Rome, everyday life is evident with washing hung conveniently above street level to dry. What drew me to take this photo were the colours of both the clothes and the building behind. The golden brown walls of the building are echoed in the golden colour of the towel, and in colour theory terms, the blue denim clothes are complementary to the golden yellow.

HANGING UP TO DRY, A LINE OF WASHING REFLECTING AND
COMPLEMENTING THE COLOURS OF ROME.

DOUBLE COMPLEMENTARY
COLOUR SCHEME

BRIGHT GOLD OVER A DARKER BLUE DOMINATES THIS ORNATE CLOCK FACE AT THE VATICAN.

NOTICE HOW THE DARK-COLOURED NUMERALS RECEDE AGAINST THE BRIGHT CREAMS AND GOLDS.

"Colour is my daylong obsession, joy and torment" – Claude Monet

THIS BRIGHTLY LIT WALL HAS MUCH GREATER TONAL DEPTH THAN ITS SHADOWY NEIGHBOUR.

GOLD FRAMES HELP THESE PAINTINGS STAND OUT FROM THE LIGHT BLUE BACKGROUND.

THIS SHUTTERED WINDOW PROVIDES TEXTURAL INTEREST AND STRONG CONTRAST TO THE WALL.

double complementary colour scheme ...

123
456

Mixing the colours

To recreate the colours I have used, add the following paste colours to white sugarpaste (rolled fondant) or use the sugarpaste I have suggested:

1 navy: bluebell (SK)
2 gold: autumn leaf (SF) and chestnut (SF) plus a touch of terracotta (SK)
3 light blue: wisteria (SK) plus a touch of violet (SK)
4 ivory: M&B ivory sugarpaste
5 terracotta: terracotta (SK) plus a touch of peach (SF)
6 denim blue: bluebell (SK)

You will need

materials

cakes: 3 round cakes 15cm (6in), 12.5cm (5in) and 10cm (4in), all at least 7.5cm (3in) high; 1 round cake 6.5cm (2½in), at least 5.5cm (2¼in) high

sugarpaste (rolled fondant): 700g (1lb 9oz) navy; 1kg (2lb 4oz) denim blue; 500g (1lb 2oz) gold; 400g (14oz) light blue; 250g (9oz) ivory; 150g (5½oz) terracotta

modelling paste: 50g (2oz) each navy, gold and terracotta; 100g (3½oz) ivory

1 quantity royal icing, plus extra icing (confectioners') sugar to thicken if needed

paste colours for painting and colouring royal icing

bronze edible lustre dust (SK)

white vegetable fat (shortening)

sugar glue

equipment

cake boards: 1 round drum 33cm (13in); 4 round hardboards 28cm (11in), 23cm (9in), 18cm (7in) and 12.5cm (5in) for clock faces; 4 round hardboards for cakes 15cm (6in), 12.5cm (5in), 10cm (4in) and 6.5cm (2½in)

9 dowels

ribbons: 15mm (⅝in) wide navy blue; 7mm (⁵⁄₁₆in) wide golden brown, light blue, cream and ivory, and non-toxic glue stick

stencils: 8in (20cm) French medallion C144; (DS); large clock C289 (DS); gem pendant C566 (DS); turn of the century mini C334 (DS)

cutters: 8.8cm (3½in) circle (FMM geometric set); funky numbers (FMM); script numbers (FMM); large numbers (FMM); block numbers (FMM); decorative designs (FMM)

piping tube (tip) no. 16 (PME)

natural sponge

paintbrush no. 4

sugar shaper

ratcheted pipe cutter (optional)

... creative clock tower

Preparation

Covering and painting the boards

As all the decoration for this cake is on cake boards, it can be done well in advance and stored – ideal if you are going to be pushed for time close to when your cake is required.

1 Create paper circle templates by drawing around the outside of all the tins (pans) used to bake the cakes.

2 Cut out the circles and place the smallest on the underside of the smallest cake board. Make sure the template is placed in the centre and then draw around it with a pencil (**Fig A**); this is to help with positioning the cake at a later stage. Repeat for the remaining three cake boards, selecting the next size up of template and board each time.

3 Cover each cake board with the appropriate colour of sugarpaste, using spacers to achieve an even finish (see Covering Boards with Sugarpaste). Place to one side to dry.

4 Working on one board at a time, dilute the paste colour(s) used to colour the sugarpaste with water.

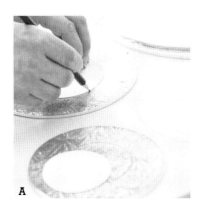

A

B

5 Take a damp natural sponge, dip it into the diluted paste colour and apply with a dabbing motion to the surface of the board. For the navy board, paint it over completely; for the golden brown board, just paint around the edges; and for the middle denim blue and top terracotta boards, paint radial patterns.

6 Once a board is painted, wash the sponge and go over the painted areas again with the clean damp sponge to blend and soften the hard edges of the colours (**Fig B**). Leave to dry thoroughly.

Stencilling

1 Colour some royal icing to match the bronze lustre dust using the suggested paste colours.

2 Adjust the consistency of the icing so that it is stiff enough not to seep under the stencil or flood the pattern once the stencil is removed, adding icing (confectioners') sugar to thicken it or cooled boiled water to soften it.

3 Place the French medallion stencils centrally on the golden brown hardboard.

4 Place a large blob of the icing in the centre of the stencil to weigh it down and prevent it from moving.

5 Take a cranked-handled palette knife and carefully begin

spreading the icing out, using long radial strokes that go right to the edge of the stencil. Remove any excess icing from the knife at the end of each stroke. For the clock face stencil, apply the icing in small sections, working around the clock face and using your hand as a central anchor (**Fig A**).

6 Once the stencil is completely covered, work towards achieving an even thickness of icing but removing any excess with more careful strokes.

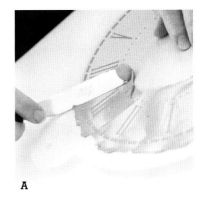

A

tip EXPERIMENT ON A SPARE PIECE OF SUGARPASTE BEFORE YOU STENCIL DIRECTLY ONTO THE COVERED HARDBOARD.

7 Once you are happy with the finish, remove the stencil by peeling it away carefully (**Fig B**).

8 Repeat for the remaining boards and stencils, changing the icing colour as appropriate.

9 Attach the matching ribbon around the edge of each board using a non-toxic glue stick (**Fig C**).

B

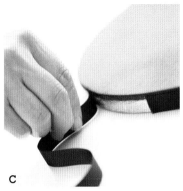

C

A

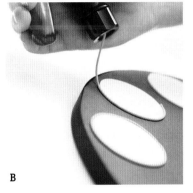

B

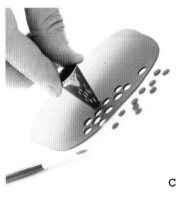

C

Adding numbers

1 To make the circles for the navy clock, knead the ivory modelling paste to warm it. Then either smear white vegetable fat over your work surface or use a non-stick workboard or mat. Roll out the paste between 1mm (¹⁄₃₂in) spacers so that it has an even thickness.

2 Press the 8.8cm (3½in) circle cutter into the paste and give it a gentle twist, without distorting the circle, to ensure that the cutter has cut cleanly through the paste (**Fig A**). Repeat.

3 Remove the excess paste from around the circles and leave them to firm up for a moment or two to prevent them from distorting.

4 Lift the circles with a palette knife and place them evenly around the edge of the covered cake drum, leaving space for the trim.

5 For the trim, soften the terracotta modelling paste, firstly by adding a little white vegetable fat to the paste to stop it getting too sticky, then by dunking it into a container of cooled boiled water and kneading. Repeat until the paste feels soft and stretchy.

6 Insert the softened paste into the barrel of the sugar shaper and add the small round disc. Squeeze out lengths of soft paste and place around the paste circles (**Fig B**). Diagonally cut the lengths to size with a craft knife so that the ends neatly abut.

7 To create the dots that mark the hours on the ivory board, thinly roll out the navy modelling paste between the 1mm (¹⁄₃₂in) spacers and use the piping tube to cut out 12 small circles (**Fig C**). Attach the dots evenly spaced around the edge of the board with sugar glue.

tip IF THE PASTE IS PICKED UP BY THE PIPING TUBE, USE A SOFT PAINTBRUSH TO PUSH IT OUT.

8 To create the numbers, thinly roll out strips of navy and gold modelling pastes between the 1mm (¹⁄₃₂in) spacers, placing a stay fresh mat or plastic food bag over the strips of paste to prevent them drying out too quickly.

... creative clock tower

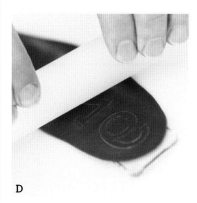

D

E

9 Leave the paste to firm up for a moment, then pick up a strip, turn it over and place on top of an appropriate-sized cutter. Roll over the paste with a rolling pin (**Fig D**), then run a finger around the shape of each number for a neat finish.

10 Pick up the number cutter and, with the paste side down, firmly tap the cutter on the side of your workboard to release the numbers (**Fig E**); it may take a couple of attempts to release them all.

11 Check the shape of the numbers and reshape as necessary before allowing them to become firm. Repeat until you have four different sets of numbers.

12 Attach each set evenly spaced around the edges of the covered cake boards. Note that not all the numbers are positioned in the same way – for example, some numbers all face one way, while others don't – so refer to the photo of the finished cake or actual clock faces for guidance.

Adding a metallic finish

Mix the edible bronze lustre dust with water to create a thick paint and use to carefully paint over the funky numbers on the navy cake board, the Roman numerals on the denim blue stencilled clock face and the gem pendant design on the small terracotta-covered board (**Fig A**).

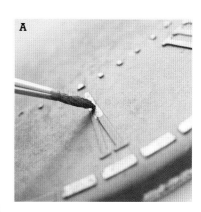

A

Making the clock hands

1 Thinly roll out navy modelling paste between 1mm (1/32in) spacers and cut out one art deco shape from the decorative designs cutter and three filigree shapes, using the same technique as for the numbers.

2 Cut the central section away from the art deco shape (**Fig A**) – this will become the pointer for the short hand of the terracotta clock.

3 Cut sections away from the three filigree shapes and reposition them to make two hands (**Fig B**).

A

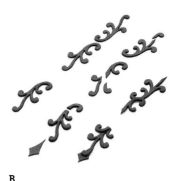

B

4 Attach with sugar glue. Add a pea-sized ball of navy paste to the centre and top with a terracotta dot.

Stage one

Carving the cakes

1 Level all but the smallest cake to 7.5cm (3in), levelling the latter to 5.5cm (2¼in) (see Levelling Cakes).

2 Make paper template circles the same size as the four cakes. Fold each circle into quarters, unfold and place on top of the appropriate cake.

3 To create a cutting guide for carving the tops of the cakes, take four cocktail sticks (toothpicks) per cake and insert one into the top edge of the cake at 45 degrees, in line with

A

one of the fold marks on the template. Insert the next opposite the first but horizontally, about 5cm (2in) from the base of the cake; on the smallest cake, mark at a height of 4cm (1½in).

4 Insert the last two cocktail sticks to mark the midway points; use the template to help with positioning and insert at the height of 6.5cm (2½in) on all except the smallest cake.

5 Take a long-bladed carving knife and, using the sticks as a guide, slice through the top of the cakes and remove the slices (**Fig A**).

6 Adjust the sloping top of the cakes as necessary, then check that the sides of the cakes are vertical, ideally using a set square.

Covering and dowelling

1 Place each cake on a hardboard cake board of matching size.

2 Cover the cakes (see Covering Cakes with Sugarpaste), paying particular attention to the finish on the lower edge. Use a smoother with a flat edge to press and cut the paste (**Fig A**) Trim the excess with a palette knife.

3 Dowel the cakes using three dowels per cake (see Dowelling Cakes). When dowelling angled cakes, each dowel position will need to be measured and the tops

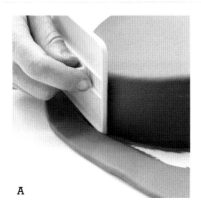

A

B

of the dowels cut at the same angle as the cake so that they will be flush with the icing – I used a ratcheted pipe cutter to do this (**Fig B**).

A

Stage two

Stacking the cakes

1 Place 1 tablespoon (15ml) royal icing on top of each cake and spread out, ensuring that the tops of the dowels are covered.

2 Using the scribed circles under each clock face, position them on top of the corresponding cakes, i.e. the smallest clock on the smallest cake etc. Allow the icing to set.

3 Finally, build the clock tower. Start at the bottom by sticking the base cake in place with royal icing. When you are happy with its position, attach the next cakes in the same way. You can rotate the cakes quite freely while the royal icing is still wet, to try out different positions, as long as you don't spend too long doing so! The idea is to give the clocks a random and haphazard look that is different from each angle viewed (**Fig A**).

... creative clock tower

You will need

cupcakes baked in orange cases (liners)

30g (generous 1oz) sugarpaste (rolled fondant) per cupcake, colours as for the main cake

circle cutter to fit the top of the cupcakes

royal icing coloured dark blue with paste colour

bronze edible lustre dust (SK)

white vegetable fat (shortening)

small clock face stencil C290 (DS)

soft dusting brush

Timely treats

These simple clock face cupcakes demonstrate how colour and contrast can influence the overall appearance of a design. The dark blue cupcake is very striking – dark colours are recessive and tend to disappear into the background, making the bronze numerals jump out and become dominant. The light blue cupcake has a surprisingly different feel, as it is less recessive. The golden cupcake in the foreground shows the effect of using the recessive navy for the numerals, and again a totally different result is created.

Adding the blue clock faces

1 Roll out a small amount of one of the light-coloured sugarpastes to a thickness of 5mm (⅕in), using spacers. Cut a circle of paste large enough to fit the top of your cupcake snugly but leave the excess paste in place, as this helps to support the stencil, allowing it to lie flat.

2 Place the clock stencil partially over the circle and carefully spread the dark blue royal icing over the relevant section of the stencil with a palette knife. Use one or two strokes, going from one side of the stencil to another to spread the icing.

3 Once the icing is of an even thickness, carefully remove the stencil. Then peel away the excess paste from around the circle.

4 Lift the stencilled circle with a palette knife and place it on top of a cupcake. Leave for a few minutes to allow the royal icing to dry – try to avoid the temptation to touch!

5 The sugarpaste circle should more or less have fallen into place, but it may be necessary to gently press down the edge of the circle so that it is in full contact with the cupcake. Doing this once the royal icing has dried prevents the pattern from being distorted or smudged.

Adding the metallic clock faces

1 Roll out one of the blue sugarpastes to a thickness of 5mm (⅕in), ideally using spacers. Place the stencil on top of the sugarpaste. Using a smoother, press down firmly onto the stencil so that the sugarpaste is forced towards the upper surface of the stencil.

2 Smear a thin layer of white vegetable fat over the surface of the sugarpaste pattern.

3 Take a large soft dusting brush and liberally dust the lustre dust over the stencil. Using your brush, remove any excess dust from the stencil; this ensures that as you lift the stencil no stray dust falls from the stencil to spoil the pattern beneath.

4 Carefully lift the stencil away from the paste to reveal the pattern.

5 Cut out circles from the stencilled pattern. Then use a cranked-handled palette knife to lift the paste and position on the cupcakes. You should be able to decorate three or four cupcakes at once using this technique.

IT IS IMPORTANT TO CAREFULLY CONSIDER THE COLOURS OF EVERY ASPECT OF YOUR CAKE - THESE LOVELY ORANGE CUPCAKE CASES PERFECTLY COMPLEMENT THE BLUES USED IN EACH DESIGN WITHOUT OVERPOWERING THE PALER GOLD AND WHITE TONES.

"Colour is born of the interpenetration of light and dark" – Sam Francis

... creative clock tower

PEACOCK
PANACHE

Colour inspiration...

The natural world is always a wonderful source of inspiration and the rich, iridescent blues and greens of a peacock are no exception. My initial idea for this project was to use a peacock feather as my colour inspiration, but I soon realized that this would create a rather dark cake. However, I remembered visiting the amazing City Palace in the heart of Jaipur, Rajasthan, and seeing the ornate but beautifully decorated doorway of the Peacock Gate, which would give me the lighter reference colours I wanted.

THE BLUES AND GREENS OF THE PEACOCK GATE OFFER AN EASY-TO-USE ANALOGOUS COLOUR SCHEME.

ANALOGOUS COLOUR SCHEME

BASE DETAIL FROM SINGAPORE'S ICONIC MERLION STATUE, MERLION PARK, MARINA BAY.

MARBLE FLOOR OF THE GOLDEN TEMPLE OF AMRITSAR, PUNJAB, INDIA.

A MOSAIC WALL DECORATION FROM ANTONI GAUDI'S PARK GÜELL, BARCELONA.

"Colour provokes a psychic vibration. Colour hides a power still unknown but real, which acts on every part of the human body" — Wassily Kandinsky

THE PEACOCK GATE IN ALL ITS GLORY, CITY PALACE OF JAIPUR.

THE RICH BLUES AND GREENS OF A PEACOCK FEATHER THAT FIRST SPARKED MY SCHEME.

CHINESE CERAMIC USING A PEACOCK-INSPIRED COLOUR PALETTE.

analogous colour scheme ...

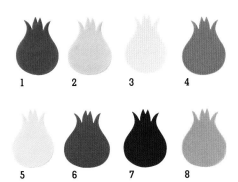

Mixing the colours

To recreate the colours I have used, add the following paste colours to white sugarpaste (rolled fondant) or use the sugarpaste I have suggested:

1 navy: M&B navy blue sugarpaste
2 blue: M&B bright blue sugarpaste
3 pale green: M&B ivory sugarpaste plus a touch of dark green and navy sugarpaste
4 green: M&B dark green and navy sugarpaste

5 pale blue-green: bluegrass (SK)
6 dark blue-green: bluegrass (SK)
7 brown: dark brown (SF)
8 golden brown: autumn leaf (SF) and chestnut (SF)

You will need

materials

cakes: 3 round cakes 18cm (7in), 12.5cm (5in) and 7.5cm (3in), all 7.5cm (3in) high

sugarpaste (rolled fondant): 600g (1lb 5oz) navy blue; 425g (15oz) blue; 800g (1lb 12oz) pale green; 500g (1lb 2oz) pale blue-green; 300g (10½oz) navy

modelling paste: 50g (2oz) each blue, navy, dark blue-green, pale green, brown, green and pale blue-green; 10g (¼oz) golden brown

edible bridal satin dusts (SK): verona green; Rimini blue; Siena brown; Florence purple

blue dust food colours: wisteria (SK); hyacinth (SK)

buttercream

royal icing, for sticking

white vegetable fat (shortening)

sugar glue

equipment

cake boards: 1 round drum 30cm (12in); 1 point to point petal drum 25.5cm (10in); 3 round hardboards 18cm (7in), 12.5cm (5in) and 7.5cm (3in)

6 dowels

15mm (⅝in) wide purple and green ribbon and non-toxic glue stick

peacock feather stencil set – C723 (DS)

cutters: peacock feather set (LC); straight frill nos. 1 and 12 (FMM); small teardrop set (LC); large teardrop set (LC); pointed ovals (LC); 5.7cm (2¼in), 5cm (2in), 4.4cm (1¾in), 3cm (1⅛in) circle (I used round pastry cutters)

sugar shaper

waxed paper

... peacock panache

Preparation

A

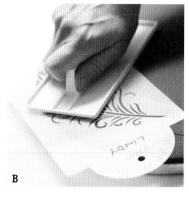

B

C

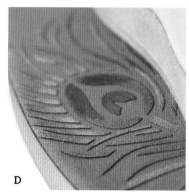

D

E

Covering and decorating the boards

1 Roll out the navy blue sugarpaste to a thickness of 5mm (⅕in), ideally using spacers, and use to cover the 30cm (12in) cake board. Trim the soft sugarpaste to size and immediately position the petal drum centrally on top of the covered board.

2 Holding a scriber like a pencil, scribe around the edges of the petal board into the soft paste (**Fig A**). Remove the petal board.

3 Position the peacock feather stencil on top of the soft paste so that the centre of the feather fits snugly between the edge of the round board and one of the indents in the scribed petal shape. Place a smoother on top of the stencil and press down firmly so that the sugarpaste is forced up to the upper surface of the stencil (**Fig B**).

4 Using either a finger or suitable paintbrush, smear a thin layer of white vegetable fat over the surface of the feather (the paste that has been forced up through the stencil).

5 Dip a paintbrush into the one of the edible dusts, knock off any excess and carefully dust over appropriate sections or part sections of the stencil, adding more dust as necessary. Repeat with a clean brush and another colour until complete (**Fig C**), using **Fig D** as a reference.

6 Using your brush, remove any excess dust from the stencil, ensuring that as you lift the stencil no stray dust falls from it to spoil the pattern beneath. Carefully peel the stencil away from the paste to reveal the pattern (**Fig E**).

7 Repeat five more times to fill the remaining indents around the edge of the navy blue board.

8 Re-trim the board with a palette knife to give a neat finish. Attach the purple ribbon to the board edge using a non-toxic glue stick.

9 Cover the petal board with blue sugarpaste and, once dry, edge with the green ribbon.

10 Using the scribed line on the decorated navy board to guide you, secure the covered petal board in place with royal icing.

Stage one

Covering the cakes

1 Stick the 18cm (7in) cake onto the cake board of the same size with buttercream and then place on waxed paper and cover the whole cake in a thin layer of buttercream using a palette knife.

2 Roll out the pale green sugarpaste and use to cover the cake.

3 Repeat for the remaining tiers, placing the cakes individually on waxed paper with the respective cake boards underneath each cake, before covering with the appropriate coloured sugarpaste. Set the cakes aside to dry.

Stage two

Assembling the cakes and adding trim to the base tier

1 Dowel the two larger cakes and stack all the cakes centrally on the covered boards (see Dowelling/ Stacking Cakes).

2 Using a paintbrush, paint a thin line of sugar glue around the base of the bottom tier of the cake.

3 Soften some of the blue modelling paste so that it is really quite soft by adding a little white vegetable fat and cooled boiled water. Place inside a sugar shaper with the medium round disc. Push down the plunger and pump with the handle to squeeze out a length of paste, then place around the base of the cake (if the paste doesn't come out easily, it isn't soft enough) (**Fig A**). Trim to fit.

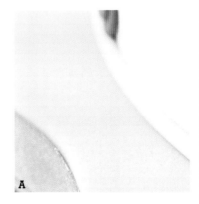

A

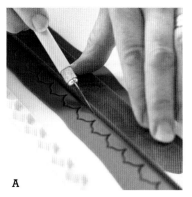

A

B

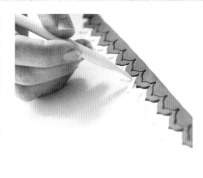

C

Adding the zig-zag decoration

1 Knead the navy modelling paste to warm it, adding a little white vegetable fat and cooled boiled water if the paste is a little dry and crumbly; you want it to be pliable but firm.

2 Thinly roll the paste out, ideally using 1mm (¹⁄₃₂in) spacers, into a 30cm (12in) long strip. Starting at one end, press the no. 1 frill cutter firmly into the paste along the strip. Remove and reposition the cutter to create a continuous pattern.

3 Position a straight edge such as a spacer on one side of the strip to give the pattern a width of 1.2cm (½in). Using a craft knife, cut the strip to size by cutting along the straight edge (**Fig A**). Remove the excess paste.

4 Roll out the dark blue-green modelling paste and use the frill cutter to cut out another strip but this time cut both sides of the pattern, aligning the pattern carefully to give a width of about 7mm (⁵⁄₁₆in) (**Fig B**). Remove the excess paste.

5 Cut strips of the same size from both the pale green and brown modelling pastes.

6 Use the strips to build the zig-zag decoration on your board, using a Dresden tool to ensure that a close fit is achieved between the layers of the design (**Fig C**).

7 Once the pattern is firm enough to lift, wrap it around the top tier of your stacked cakes, securing in place with sugar glue. Cut away any excess pattern and adjust the fit as necessary.

8 To create a neat and more interesting finish, roll out the blue modelling paste and cut a further strip of pattern using the cutter. Cut one edge straight close to the edge of the design. Wrap it around the base of the top tier (**Fig D**).

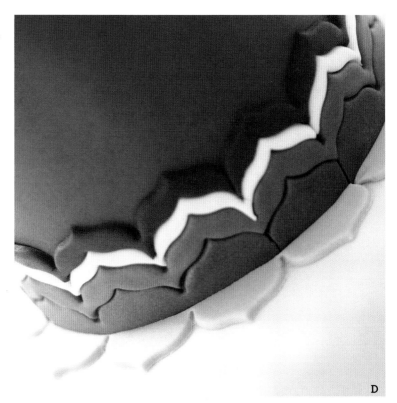

D

Creating the peacock feather

1 For the decorative peacock feathers on the middle tier, separately roll out the appropriate modelling pastes, ideally between 1mm (1/32in) spacers. Using the peacock cutter set and the smallest teardrop cutter from the small teardrop set, cut out enough shapes for seven pattern repeats (**Fig A**).

tip USE A STAY FRESH MAT TO PREVENT YOUR ROLLED-OUT PASTE FROM DRYING OUT.

2 To make the feather stem, use the cutter from the peacock feather set to cut large teardrop shapes from dark blue-green modelling paste, then cut across the tip of the shapes, keeping the smallest section (**Fig B**). Allow the paste shapes to firm up a little.

3 To mark the position of the feather on the middle tier, make a paper collar by cutting a strip of waxed paper and taping it so that it fits snugly around the tier. Slip the collar vertically up and off the cake. Press the collar flat to crease the folds, then make two more folds equidistant apart so that when the collar is unfolded it has six vertical evenly spaced fold lines. Slip the collar back onto the cake, position the creases so that they line up with the widest parts of the petal board and mark the position of all six creased lines with a scriber.

A

4 Attach the feather stems in place on top of the scribed line using sugar glue. Then layer and build up the six peacock feathers as shown (**Fig C**).

5 The seventh feather is for the top of the cake. Glue the relevant sections in place and then set aside to dry thoroughly.

6 Cut out six 3cm (1⅛in) wide circles from the pale green modelling paste, cut each in half and then attach to the top of the base tier, one half either side of each feather (**Fig C**).

B

C

... peacock panache

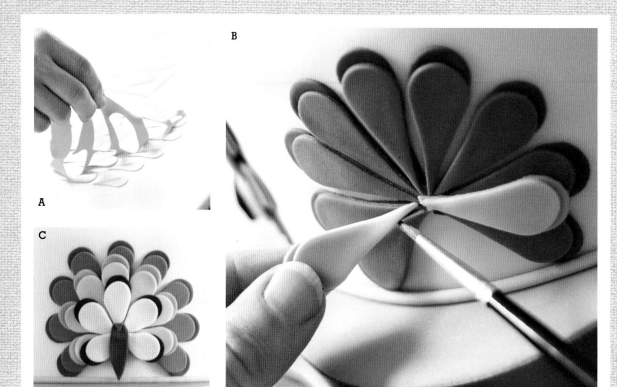

A

B

C

Creating the abstract peacocks

1 For the peacock decoration on the base tier, separately roll out the dark blue-green and green modelling pastes, ideally between 1mm (1/32in) spacers. Use the 4cm (1½in) teardrop cutter from the large teardrop set to cut out 54 teardrop shapes from each paste colour.

2 Stack the green teardrops on top of the dark blue-green ones so that 3mm (1/8in) of the top of the dark green teardrops is clearly visible.

3 Using nine of these stacked shapes for each peacock, attach in place on the cake in a fan shape, as seen in **Fig B**, ensuring that the fan is positioned directly below the peacock feathers of the middle tier.

4 Cut out 42 blue and pale blue-green modelling paste teardrops (**Fig A**). Stack as in step 3, then attach seven stacked shapes to the top of the fan shapes (**Fig B**).

5 Using the smallest teardrop cutter from the large teardrop set, cut out 30 brown and 30 pale green teardrops, stack as before and then add five to each fan.

6 Cut six pointed ovals from navy modelling paste, curl one point over to symbolize a head and stick in place (**Fig C**).

A

Adding the top decoration

1 Thinly roll out the blue, pale green and pale blue-green modelling pastes. Use the three largest circle cutters to cut out one circle of the appropriate size from each paste colour (**Fig A**).

2 Stack as shown (**Fig B**) and attach to the top of the cake (**Fig C**).

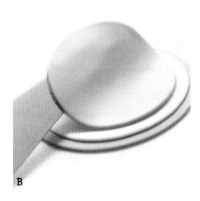

B

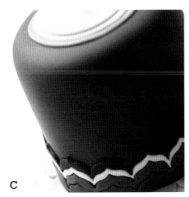

C

Stage three

The prepared modelling paste feather for the top of the cake will be affected by moisture in the atmosphere, so to prevent the feather 'wilting', add it to the top of the cake at the last moment, using a small amount of firm royal icing and supporting the feather while the icing dries.

Fan-tastic cookies

For these eye-catching fan cookies I have adapted the design from the bottom tier of the main cake. Like the cake, the colours used are all from the same part of the colour wheel, so they look pleasing on the eye. Out of the four backgrounds I have chosen to display the cookie, I think the most striking is the brown because it allows the other colours to speak for themselves. Brown is a warm neutral colour and as such does not appear on the colour wheel, since it is a mixture of all three primary colours.

1 Create fans on the cookies in the same way as for the peacocks on the main cake, using modelling paste and large teardrop cutters. Use piping gel to stick the teardrops in place.

2 Roll out some navy sugarpaste between 5mm (⅛in) spacers and emboss it, once for each cookie, using the appropriate lace embosser. Use the cookie cutter to cut out the embossed shapes so that it forms the handle of the fan.

3 Using a craft knife, cut away the excess paste above the embossed patterns in a smooth arc.

4 Attach in place on the cookies with piping gel.

tip NEUTRAL COLOURS SUCH AS THE BROWN IN THIS EXAMPLE OFTEN WORK WELL AS BACKGROUND COLOURS BECAUSE THEY TEND NOT TO AFFECT OTHER COLOURS TOO DRASTICALLY, AS DEMONSTRATED HERE.

analogous colour scheme ...

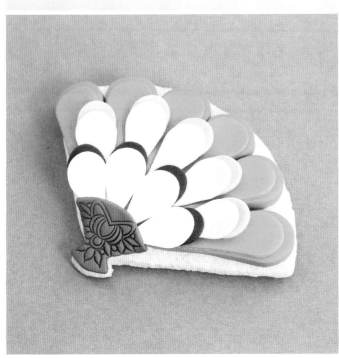

THE BACKGROUNDS I HAVE SELECTED ARE STILL WITHIN THE SAME COLOUR PALETTE AS THE COOKIE AND CAKE, BUT IT IS THE PROPORTION OF THE COLOUR THAT AFFECTS THE OVERALL APPEARANCE. COMPARE THE COOKIE ON THE BLUE BACKGROUND TO THAT ON THE GREEN AND SEE HOW IN THE BLUE LINE OF TEARDROPS THE BLUES APPEAR TO BE MORE PROMINENT ON THE GREEN THAN ON THE BLUE BACKGROUND.

"Colours are promiscuous. They get infected by their neighbours" – Paul Richard

... peacock panache

BIRDHOUSE
CHIC

Colour inspiration...
Here, pretty pastel shades of pinks, purples, blues and greens blend together beautifully, epitomizing warm sunlit days. I chose as my colour reference a print of a watercolour painting with many more colours and shades than I have featured in the cake. I have selected colours that complement each other and work together, such as the turquoise of the mug's handle and the lime green of the shadow. In colour theory terms, I have chosen a combination of cool colours.

COOL COLOUR SCHEME

'Teacups' card by Phoenix Trading © Tina Schneider

CARDS ARE OFTEN A FABULOUS SOURCE OF COLOUR INSPIRATION, AS WITH THIS LOVELY WATERCOLOUR BY TINA SCHNEIDER.

cool colour scheme ...

DIANTHUS FLOWERS, LIVING POMPOMS OF VIBRANT ACID LIME GREEN.

APPLE BLOSSOM WITH ITS MYRIAD VARIATIONS ON PINK.

"I found I could say things with colours that I couldn't say in any other way – things that I had no words for" – Georgia O'Keeffe

PASTEL-COLOURED BEACH HUTS AT WELLS-NEXT-THE-SEA, NORFOLK.

THE CANDY PINK TONES OF A SHAGGY ORNAMENTAL POPPY.

cool colour scheme ...

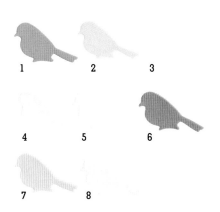

Mixing the Colours

To recreate the colours I have used, add the following paste colours to white sugarpaste (rolled fondant) or use the sugarpaste I have suggested:

1 purple: M&B amethyst and white sugarpaste plus red extra (SF) and rose (SK)

2 blue: gentian (SK) plus a touch of vine (SK)

3 pale blue: as for blue above

4 green: vine (SK) plus a touch of bluebell (SK)

5 pale green: as for green above

6 pink: red extra (SF) plus a touch of rose (SK)

7 pale pink: as for pink above

8 very pale pink: as for pale pink above plus more white

You will need

materials

23cm (9in) square cake, 7.5cm (3in) high

sugarpaste (rolled fondant): 450g (1lb) purple; 500g (1lb 2oz) each pale green and pale pink; 900g (2lb) pale blue

25g (1oz) pastillage coloured purple

modelling paste: 200g (7oz) pale green; 50g (2oz) each very pale pink, pale blue and purple; 25g (1oz) deep purple

royal icing, coloured very pale pink, green, blue and pink using the suggested paste colours NB the colours are darker than the sugarpaste of the same colour with the exception of pale pink

buttercream

white vegetable fat (shortening)

sugar glue

equipment

cake boards: 1 square drum 8cm (7in); 2 square thin hardboards 15cm (6in); 1 round spare board for turning cake at least 25.5cm (10in)

15mm (⅝in) wide purple ribbon and non-toxic glue stick

sugar shaper

cutters: five-petal flower (PME); 3.6cm (1⅜in) circle; straight frill set 1–4 (FMM)

no. 2 piping tube (tip) (PME)

stencils: cherry blossom (LC); vintage botanical (LC); scroll set (DS)

lace motif (HP set 19) stick embosser

waxed paper

... birdhouse chic

Preparation

1 Cover the 18cm (7in) square cake drum with the purple sugarpaste, using 5mm (⅛in) spacers in order to achieve an even finish (see Covering Cakes with Sugarpaste). Set aside to dry thoroughly.

2 Knead the pale green modelling paste to warm, adding a little white vegetable fat and cooled boiled water if necessary to make it soft and pliable. Roll out two-thirds between 1mm (½in) spacers and use to cover one of the 15cm (6in) hardboard cake boards. Cover the other hardboard with the remaining pale green paste, then set aside to dry.

3 Soften the purple pastillage by adding a little white vegetable fat and cooled boiled water. Place inside a sugar shaper with the large round disc. Push down the plunger and pump using the handle to squeeze out a length of paste (**Fig A**). Cut into at least two 9cm (3½in) lengths, one for the perch and one as a spare (although strong, pastillage is also very brittle). Place on a foam pad and allow to dry thoroughly.

tip IF YOU DON'T HAVE A SUGAR SHAPER, ROLL THE PERCH BY HAND USING A SMOOTHER TO HELP YOU ACHIEVE AN EVEN FINISH.

A

4 To create the flowers, cut five-petal flowers from the thinly rolled-out pale pink modelling paste and place in cupped formers to dry (**Fig B**). Once dry, pipe large dots of very pale pink royal icing in the centre of each flower using the no. 2 piping tube, then once this has dried, pipe small dots around the centre.

B

tip YOU CAN BUY READY-MADE POLYSTYRENE FORMERS, BUT THEY ARE EASILY MADE FROM FOIL CUPPED OVER THE TOP OF A ROUND PASTRY CUTTER, CUP OR GLASS.

Stage one

Carving the cake

1 Cut out a 20cm (8in) square from paper as a template.

2 Level the cake (see Levelling Cakes), then place the square template on top, securing in place with cocktail sticks (toothpicks). Using a sharp carving knife, cut vertically around the template to create a perfectly square cake. Cut the cake in half to give you two 20cm x 10cm (8in x 4in) pieces of cake. Make another cut perpendicular to the first 5cm (2in) in from one edge. This reduces the longer sections of cake to 15cm (6in) and gives you two additional 10cm x 5cm (4in x 2in) pieces.

3 Spread buttercream over the top of one of the larger pieces of cake and stack the second on top. Spread buttercream over the top of the stack and then add both smaller sections of cake, using buttercream to sandwich them firmly together (**Fig A**).

A

4 Enlarge the bird box template at 200% so that the width becomes 15cm (6in) and the height 21cm (8¼in), then cut out two of the templates from waxed paper. Attach to the cake sides with cocktail sticks, ensuring that they are perfectly aligned with each other.

5 Holding the carving knife at right angles to the templates, carve away the excess cake to give you the shape of the bird box (**Fig B**). Remove the cocktail sticks and templates.

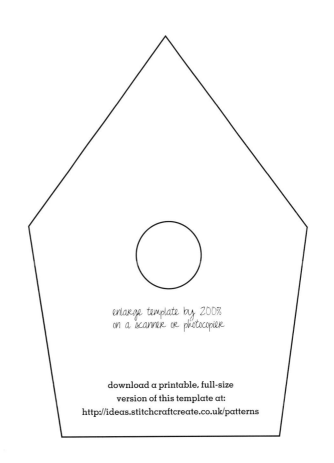

enlarge template by 200% on a scanner or photocopier

download a printable, full-size version of this template at:
http://ideas.stitchcraftcreate.co.uk/patterns

B

Stage two

Covering the green sides

1 For the green sides of the cake, firstly colour about a third of the royal icing a slightly darker shade of green than the pale green sugarpaste.

2 Knead the green sugarpaste to make it warm and pliable, then roll out about two-thirds to a thickness of 5mm (⅛in), ideally between spacers. Place the cherry blossom stencil on top of the paste and use a palette knife to spread the green royal icing evenly over the stencil (**Fig A**). Then lift the stencil to reveal the pattern (**Fig B**).

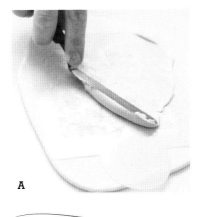

A

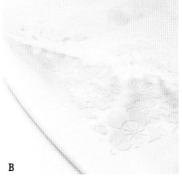

B

tip THE SECRET TO SUCCESS IS THE CORRECT ICING CONSISTENCY - TOO SOFT AND IT WILL FLOOD UNDER THE STENCIL AND SPOIL THE PATTERN; TOO STIFF AND IT TENDS TO BE UNEVEN AND CRACK.

... birdhouse chic

3 Use a palette knife to cut around three sides of the stencilled pattern, leaving one shorter edge uncut. Spread buttercream over one side of the cake – meanwhile, the stencilled pattern should dry – then carefully pick up the patterned paste and use a smoother to press the patterned paste onto the freshly spread buttercream (**Fig C**).

C

D

4 Use a palette knife to cut the excess green paste flush with the roof of the bird box (**Fig D**).

tip IT IS VERY IMPORTANT THAT THE ROYAL ICING IS DRY BEFORE YOU DO THIS, OR THE PATTERN WILL SMUDGE!

Covering the front and back

A

B

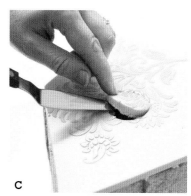

C

1 Cut two 25.5cm (10in) squares of waxed paper. Knead the blue sugarpaste to warm, then roll out about two-thirds to a depth of 5mm (⅕in), ideally using spacers. Pick up the paste and place it on a square of waxed paper, flipping the paste over so that the underside is uppermost.

2 Cover the front of the cake with a thin layer of buttercream, then carefully place the buttercreamed surface on top of the rolled-out sugarpaste. Using a palette knife, cut the blue sugarpaste to size, ensuring that the palette knife is flush with the cake to achieve a straight cut (**Fig A**).

3 Place the second sheet of waxed paper and the spare cake board on top of the cake and flip through 180 degrees so that the blue sugarpaste is uppermost. Remove the top sheet of waxed paper.

4 Place the front template on top of the cake, then holding the circle cutter directly above the circle on the template (**Fig B**), quickly slide the template away before using the cutter to cut a circle through the sugarpaste. Don't remove the paste at this stage.

5 Place the vintage botanical stencil on top of the cake, adjusting as necessary, then spread blue royal icing evenly over the stencil. Remove the excess icing before lifting the stencil to reveal the pattern.

6 While the royal icing is still wet, remove the cut sugarpaste circle with a palette knife (**Fig C**). If necessary, take a damp paintbrush and use to tidy up the royal icing around the edge of the circle.

7 Once the royal icing has set, which only takes a few minutes, replace the sugarpaste circle with a circle cut from 2mm (1⁄16in) thick deep purple modelling paste.

8 Stand the cake upright and cover the back with buttercream and sugarpaste as for the front.

Covering the roof

1 Cover the two sides of the roof with buttercream and place the prepared covered 15cm (6in) square hardboards, covered-side down, onto the buttercream (**Fig A**). Position so that the tops of the boards are as close as possible to one another and the sides are parallel with the cake.

2 Soften some of the pale pink modelling paste by adding a little white vegetable fat and cooled boiled water. Place inside the sugar shaper with the large round disc. Push down the plunger and pump using the handle to squeeze out a length of paste. Place along the top of the roof to fill the gap between the boards and to create the ridge. Using a smoother, flatten each side of the paste sausage so that it is flush with the top of the roof.

3 Cover the board edges with cooled boiled water or sugar glue.

4 Roll out the pink sugarpaste so that it is at least 15cm (6in) wide x 30.5cm (12in) long. Pick the paste up over your rolling pin and carefully drape over the entire roof top (**Fig B**). Trim to size with a palette knife.

5 Use one of the scroll designs to stencil a pattern on each side of the roof using the pink royal icing.

6 Soften some of the blue modelling paste and place inside the sugar shaper with the medium round disc. Squeeze out four 12.5cm (5in) lengths and leave to firm up for a minute or

A

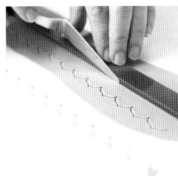

B

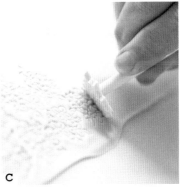

C

D

two. Paint sugar glue along the top edges of the front and back sections of the cake, where the blue paste abuts the roof, and position the lengths of paste over the glue to neaten the join. Trim to fit with a craft knife.

7 For the textured green trim on the front of the roof, thinly roll out some green modelling paste and use a stick embosser to add texture (**Fig C**), making sure you apply the same pressure each time you emboss so that the pattern has an even depth. Cut the paste into four strips to fit with a craft knife, attach with sugar glue and trim.

8 For the ridge decoration, thinly roll out the purple modelling paste between 1mm (⅟₃₂in) spacers. Press the frill cutter firmly into the paste. Create a strip by cutting a straight line 1cm (⅜in) from the pattern using a straight edge such as a spacer and a palette knife (**Fig D**). Cut a second exactly the same width and attach to form the ridge, as seen in the main photo.

9 To disguise the join at the very top of the ridge, add a purple modelling paste trim created using the sugar shaper and medium round disc.

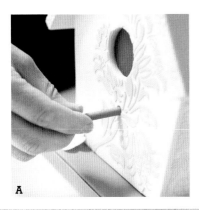

A

The finishing touches

1 Add the ribbon to the edges of the prepared cake board using a non-toxic glue stick. Then transfer the cake carefully to the centre of the board.

2 Attach the flowers to the cake and board with a little royal icing.

3 Insert the perch about 2.5cm (1in) below the purple hole (**Fig A**).

... birdhouse chic

You will need

cupcakes baked in purple cases (liners)

30g (generous 1oz) sugarpaste (rolled fondant) per cupcake, colours as for the main cake

royal icing coloured pink, blue, green and purple with paste colour

modelling paste colours as for the main cake

cutters: circle to fit the top of the cupcakes; bird silhouette set (LC)

cherry blossom stencil (LC)

sugar glue

Dove dainties

For these pretty cupcakes I have chosen to team up two colours and show how the proximity and proportion of one colour to another colour alters the feel or the perception of the colours used. Pastel blues and pinks always look good together, but see what happens when the proportions of each colour change. When the blue bird is on the pink cupcake it has a completely different feel to the pink bird on the blue cupcake, and which you prefer is always very much a personal choice.

1 Roll out a small amount of one of the coloured sugarpastes to a thickness of 5mm (⅕in) using spacers. Cut a circle of paste large enough to snugly fit the top of your cupcake, but leave the excess paste in place, as this helps to support the stencil, allowing it to lie flat.

2 Position the cherry blossom stencil over the circle and carefully spread some royal icing coloured a shade darker than the sugarpaste over the relevant section of the stencil with a cranked-handled palette knife.

3 Once the icing is of an even thickness, carefully remove the stencil, then peel away the excess paste from around the circle.

4 Lift the stencilled circle with a palette knife and place it on top of a cupcake. Leave for a few minutes to allow the royal icing to dry – try to avoid the temptation to touch it!

5 The sugarpaste circle should more or less have fallen into place, but it may be necessary to gently press down the edge so that it is in full contact with the cupcake. Doing this once the royal icing has dried prevents the pattern from being distorted or smudged.

6 Repeat using the different sugarpaste colours and coloured royal icing.

7 Thinly roll out the modelling paste colours and cut out a selection of bird silhouettes. Attach to the cupcakes with sugar glue.

Colour is, on the evidence of language alone, very bound up with the feelings – Joanna Field

I LOVE THE COMBINATION OF PURPLE AND GREEN AND HAVE CHOSEN HERE TO USE THE PURPLE IN A SLIGHTLY DARKER SHADE TO ILLUSTRATE THAT COLOURS ALWAYS APPEAR MORE VIBRANT ON A DARK BACKGROUND - THE PALE GREEN SILHOUETTE REALLY STANDS OUT AS YOU CAN SEE. CONVERSELY, THE PURPLE BIRD SEEMS QUITE DULL ON THE PALE GREEN BACKGROUND.

... birdhouse chic

COLOUR CRESCENDO

Colour inspiration...

I have always been drawn to bright vibrant colours, so it was hardly surprising when I stumbled upon a book of San Francisco-based fine artist/designer Rex Ray's in a contemporary art gallery that I instantly fell in love with his work. The artwork I have selected as my inspiration is called *Chrysotomontum*. Although my cake has a completely different theme, I have tried to use the same balance of colours as Ray, choosing a deep orange as the background and a mixture of dark blue, red, rich yellow, lime greens and so on for the decoration.

REX RAY ALWAYS USES A WONDERFUL PALETTE OF FLAMBOYANT COLOURS, WHICH IN TURN CREATES A STRIKING CAKE.

Chrysotomontum © Rex Ray, 2005 www.rexray.com

POLYCHROMATIC COLOUR SCHEME

JAZZY PINK GERANIUM CREATING A SPLASH OF VIBRANT COLOUR.

THE RICH, PUNCHY COLOURS OF AN ORANGE-FLOWERED BEGONIA.

A CANDLELIT TEA LIGHT, A STRIKING EXAMPLE OF BLACK AND WHITE.

NATURE'S COLOUR PALETTE ON DISPLAY AT A SINGAPORE MARKET.

WINTER SUN IN WOODLAND POETICALLY CONTRASTS LIGHT WITH DARK.

"Colour is like a volatile radio-active element, it is extremely powerful and should be handled very, very carefully" – Sean Adams

polychromatic colour scheme ...

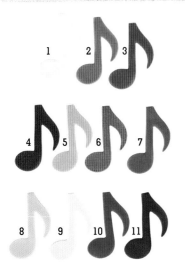

Mixing the colours

To recreate the colours I have used, add the following paste colours to white sugarpaste (rolled fondant) or use the sugarpaste I have suggested:

1 ivory: M&B sugarpaste

2 mid orange: mixed dark vibrant orange sugarpaste plus white sugarpaste and sunflower (SK)

3 dark vibrant orange: M&B orange sugarpaste plus red extra (SF)

4 red: red extra (SF)

5 deep yellow: sunflower (SK)

6 deep muted pink: M&B dark pink sugarpaste plus claret (SF) and pink (SF)

7 dark green: M&B dark green sugarpaste plus bluebell (SK)

8 mid green: vine (SK) plus a touch of mixed dark green paste

9 lime green: vine (SK) and sunflower (SK) plus a touch of mixed dark green paste

10 navy blue: M&B sugarpaste

11 black: M&B sugarpaste plus black extra (SF)

You will need

materials

cakes: 2 round cakes 12.5cm (5in), 7.5cm (3in) high; 1 round cake 10cm (4in), 10cm (4in) high

sugarpaste (rolled fondant): 500g (1lb 2oz) each ivory and deep muted pink; 750g (1lb 10oz) dark vibrant orange

modelling paste: 100g (3½oz) black; 25g (1oz) each dark vibrant orange, dark green, ivory, deep muted pink, navy blue, mid orange, mid green and lime green; 50g (2oz) each deep yellow and red

small amount of pastillage

royal icing, for sticking

black paste colour for colouring royal icing

buttercream

sugar glue

equipment

cake boards: 1 round cake drum 25.5cm (10in); 1 round hardboard 10cm (4in)

15mm (⅝in) wide pink velvet ribbon and non-toxic glue stick

3 long dowels (at least 15cm/6in)

cutters: music and sport tappits set (FMM); mini musical notes from disco dancers set (PC); musical notes set (LC); Persian petal set 1 (LC); curled leaf set (LC); leaf from large daisies (PC); daisy marguerite (PME); flat floral collection set 2 (LC)

moulds: 6mm (¼in) perfect pearls BR129 (FI); daisy set FL288 (FI); small flower mould set 1 FL127 (FI); roses galore FL248 (FI); mini misc flowers FL107 (FI); daisy centre stamp set (JEM)

piping tubes (tips): nos. 1.5, 16 and 17 (PME)

embossers: flower set 1 (FMM); flower set 10 (HP)

colour-topped dressmakers' pins

long, thin straight edge, e.g. carving knife

sugar shaper

waxed paper

… colour crescendo

Preparation

Covering the board and adding the ivory piano keys

1 Make a round paper template the same size as the cake drum and fold the circle in half four times, lining up the edges as accurately as you possibly can (**Fig A**).

2 Roll out the ivory sugarpaste to a thickness of 5mm (⅛in), ideally using spacers, and use to cover the cake drum.

3 Unfold the circle, which should now be divided into 16 equal segments, and place on top of the soft sugarpaste covering the cake drum.

4 Using dressmakers' pins, pin the template to the board to prevent it moving, then prick 16 holes through the template to mark the sections, making sure that these holes are at least 6cm (2⅜in) in from the outer edge (**Fig B**). Once complete, remove the pins and template.

5 Take a long, thin straight edge – I used a carving knife – and line up the pin pricks across the covered board, then carefully mark the 16 triangles, taking care not to cut completely through the paste (**Fig C**).

6 Take a palette knife and divide each segment in half, then halve each half to create four keys in each section, making 64 keys and eight octaves in total (**Fig D**).

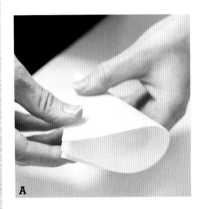

A

B

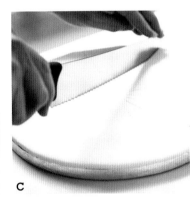

C

D

Creating the treble clef and notes

1 To create the treble clef, thinly roll out a small strip of black modelling paste between 1mm (½2in) spacers. Leave the paste to firm up for a moment or two, then pick up the strip, turn it over and place on top of the tappits cutter. Roll over the paste with a rolling pin, then run a finger around the shape to achieve a neat finish (**Fig A**).

2 Pick up the cutter and firmly tap it, paste-side down, onto the side of your work board to release the treble clef – it may take a couple of attempts.

3 Check the shape and reshape as necessary before allowing the paste to become firm. Place on a foam pad to dry completely.

4 Roll out the black paste again, this time more thinly, and cut out small black notes using the musical note cutters from the disco set. Place on foam to dry.

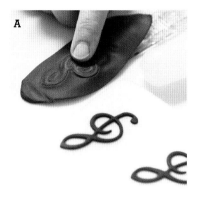

A

B

5 Colour the pastillage black, ideally using black extra (SF) paste colour, and roll out to a thickness of 2mm (⅙in). Cut out the smallest and the largest notes from the musical note set, i.e. the 4.5cm (1¾in) and 7cm (2¾in) high notes. Place on foam and allow to dry thoroughly.

6 Once the notes are thoroughly dry, colour a little royal icing black and stick the small quaver to the larger one as pictured (**Fig B**).

tip ALTHOUGH STRONG ONCE DRY, PASTILLAGE IS ALSO VERY BRITTLE, SO MAKE A FEW SPARE NOTES IN CASE OF BREAKAGES.

Stage one

Covering the cakes

1 Level both the 12.5cm (5in) cakes (see Levelling Cakes), spread buttercream over the top of one cake and stack the other on top. Check that the sides of your cake are all vertical and adjust if necessary, then spread a thin layer of buttercream over the whole cake to adhere the sugarpaste.

2 Knead the dark vibrant orange sugarpaste to warm it, then roll it out into a rectangular shape using 5mm (⅕in) spacers. Turn the paste over and cut it into a 20cm (8in) wide x 50cm (20in) long rectangle. Place the cake on its side on the paste so that the base is flush with one long edge. Roll

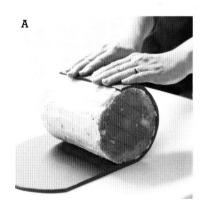

A

up the cake in the paste, trim the paste as necessary to create a neat, straight join and rub closed using the heat of your hand – the join is easily disguised by the decoration (**Fig A**).

3 Stand your cake upright on waxed paper and fold the sugarpaste over the top of the cake, cutting away the excess with scissors. Use a smoother to smooth the sides and top of the cake.

4 Level the 10cm (4in) cake and place on the 10cm (4in) cake board, then cover the cake and board with the deep muted pink sugarpaste (see Covering Cakes with Sugarpaste). Allow the sugarpaste on the cake to crust over.

... colour crescendo

Stage two

Adding the music staves

1 Soften some dark vibrant orange modelling paste so that it is really quite soft. Do this by firstly kneading in some white vegetable fat and then dunking the paste into cooled boiled water and re-kneading. Repeat until it feels soft and stretchy. Place the paste together with the no 1.5 piping tube into the sugar shaper.

2 Take a fine paintbrush and some sugar glue and paint freehand staves ending in scrolls on the cake, referring to the step photo (**Fig A**) and that of the main cake for guidance.

3 Squeeze out a length of paste from the sugar shaper (if the paste doesn't come out easily, the paste isn't soft enough) and place it over a section of the painted glue pattern, using a paintbrush to aid placement (**Fig B**). Cut to length on the cake using a palette or craft knife. Review the shape and adjust as necessary, using your paintbrush to give the shape smooth curves. Repeat for the remaining four staves.

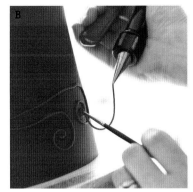

A

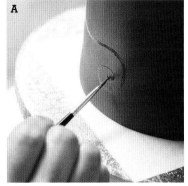

B

Dowelling and stacking the cake

Carefully place the covered orange cake onto the prepared board. Using three dowels, dowel the orange cake (see Dowelling Cakes). Then attach the pink tier in place using royal icing.

Adding the black piano keys

1 For the felt trim on the keys, soften some dark green modelling paste so that it is soft and stretchy, then insert the softened paste into the barrel of the sugar shaper and add the small ribbon disc. Squeeze out a length of soft paste and place on the keys around the base of the orange cake. Cut to size with a craft knife so that the ends neatly abut.

2 Roll out the black modelling paste between 5mm (⅛in) spacers and cut out a 3.6cm (1⅜in) wide strip. Next, make marks every 6mm (¼in) along the strip with a ruler and craft knife. Using a palette knife, cut the strip into 6mm (¼in) wide fingers (**Fig A**).

3 Separate the fingers and squeeze one end of each between two spacers, or smoothers, to taper the note slightly – this will allow it to fit onto the circular ivory keys (**Fig B**).

4 Using the craft knife, cut away a triangular wedge from the front of each note (**Fig C**).

5 Position your black keys in place, referring to the photo detail for placement (**Fig D**), or an actual keyboard if necessary.

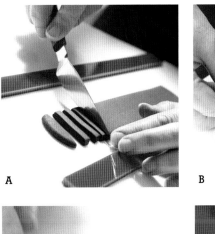

A

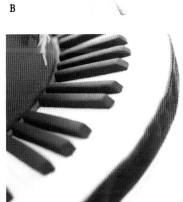

B

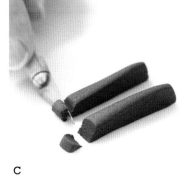

C

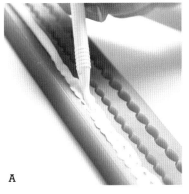

D

Creating the pearls

1 To create the two strings of pearls, knead some ivory modelling paste to warm it, then roll into a long sausage approximately 7mm (⁵⁄₁₆in) thick. Place the paste on top of the 6mm (¼in) section of the perfect pearls mould, then press into the mould with firstly your fingers and then the back of a Dresden tool (**Fig A**).

2 Using a palette knife, cut away the excess paste and then release the pearls by flexing the mould along its length so that the pearls fall out without breaking or distorting (**Fig B**). Cut the string to 25.5cm (10in) long and attach in position on the base tier.

3 Repeat to cut a 10cm (4in) string of pearls, then stick in position on the top tier, as shown in the main photo.

A

B

... colour crescendo

Creating decorative shapes

1 To create the Persian petal shapes, thinly roll out the dark green modelling paste, ideally between 1mm (1/32in) spacers. Take the multi petal daisy embosser from the flower embossing set (FMM) and, holding it between your thumb and index finger at right angles to the paste, press into the soft paste. Repeat, leaving space between the flowers.

2 Take the large 4.5cm (1¾in) wide Persian petal cutter and cut out shapes, as shown (**Fig A**). Repeat using the same paste but with the small flower embosser and a 2.5cm (1in) wide petal cutter. Repeat again using the same cutter but with the deep muted pink modelling paste and the five-petal flower embosser.

3 Cut some curled leaves from thinly rolled-out navy blue modelling paste. Place the shapes under a stay fresh mat or plastic food bag to prevent them drying out.

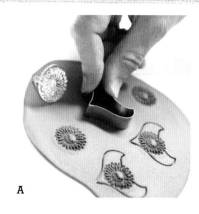

A

Creating moulded flowers

1 To make the large moulded daisy, knead a small amount of ivory modelling paste to warm it, then roll a small ball of paste smaller than the centre of the flower mould. Press into the centre of the mould using a ball tool; ideally, the paste should just line this section so that when the next colour is added it doesn't spread into the surrounding area (**Fig A**).

2 Roll a ball of mid orange modelling paste slightly larger than the mould cavity. Place in the mould, ensuring that the sugar surface in the mould is perfectly smooth. Push the paste firmly into the mould.

3 Using a palette knife, remove the excess paste so that the back of the mould is flat, as shown (**Fig B**). Then using your fingers and/or a Dresden tool, make sure that the edge of each petal is properly defined by drawing the excess paste between petals into the centre.

A

B

4 Carefully flex the mould to release the paste. If the coloured centre of the flower has spread to the surrounding petals, you need to add less paste into the centre next time.

5 Repeat using different moulds and different modelling paste colours, as shown in the photos of the finished cake.

6 Using sugar glue, start attaching the moulded flowers and the embossed decorative shapes to the cake, referring to the detail photo of the finished cake for guidance on where to place.

tip IF YOU ARE NOT GETTING ENOUGH DETAIL, CHECK THAT YOU ARE PRESSING THE PASTE FIRMLY AND THAT IT'S NOT TOO STIFF.

Creating daisy leaves

To create the daisy leaves, roll out the mid green and lime green modelling pastes very thinly and cut out daisy leaves, making sure that your modelling paste is firm enough to create them. Attach to the cake giving each leaf a little movement – do this by sticking sections only of the leaf to the cake, allowing other parts to come away from the cake surface.

Cutter flowers and dots

1 Create navy and yellow two-layer flowers using the two smallest cutters from the daisy marguerite set and cut out rounded eight-petal flowers using the flat floral collection set and mid orange modelling paste. Attach to the cake and add flower centres created using the daisy centre stamp set and yellow modelling paste.

2 Thinly roll out some black modelling paste and cut out black dots using the nos. 16 and 17 piping tubes. Attach a few around the flower patterns, as shown in the detail photo of the finished cake.

Adding the notes

Attach the treble clef and musical notes to the staves as shown. Using royal icing coloured black and pins to secure, attach the top notes to the cake. Remove the pins once the icing has dried.

Finishing touches

1 Using a sugar shaper fitted with a small ribbon disc and softened red modelling paste, add an edible ribbon to the exposed join between the two tiers of the cake.

2 Finally, attach a pink velvet ribbon to the edge of the cake drum using a non-toxic glue stick.

... colour crescendo

You will need

cupcakes baked in black and pink cases (liners)

30g (generous 1oz) sugarpaste (rolled fondant) per cupcake, colours as for the main cake plus black

modelling paste, colours as for the main cake plus black

circle cutter to fit the top of the cupcakes

moulds: roses galore FL248 (FI); mini misc flowers FL107 (FI)

cutters: music and sport tappits set (FMM); mini musical notes from disco dancer set (PC)

sugar glue

Keynote cupcakes

These pretty musical cupcakes illustrate the effect colour balance and contrast have on the overall appearance of the cupcakes. The flowers remain the same on each cupcake but the background colour changes, as does the treble clef and quaver, switching from black to white. The cupcake that appeals to me most is the one with the dark pink background and black note. However, as explained in the introduction to this book, we all see colour differently, so I assume you will have your personal favourite that isn't necessarily the same as mine!

1 Cut treble clefs and notes from thinly rolled-out modelling paste as for the main cake, then set aside and allow to dry.

2 Roll out the sugarpaste colours to a thickness of 5mm (⅛in) using spacers. Cut circles of paste large enough to fit the tops of your cupcakes snugly. Position the paste circles on top of your cupcakes.

3 Use a cutting wheel to emboss staves into the soft sugarpaste, as shown.

4 Make moulded flowers as for the main cake and attach them to the cupcakes with sugar glue.

5 Finally, attach the treble clefs and notes in place on the cupcakes.

tip LEAVE YOUR ROLLED-OUT MODELLING PASTE FOR A FEW MOMENTS TO HARDEN SLIGHTLY BEFORE CUTTING OUT FLIMSY SHAPES.

"Why do two colours, put next to each other, sing? Can we really explain this? No" – Pablo Picasso

SOME OF THE HOT, RICH, JAZZY COLOURS FROM THE MAIN CAKE ARE TEAMED WITH BLACK AND WHITE TO MAKE A SET OF CUPCAKES 'CON BRIO'! BLACK AND ITS OPPOSITE WHITE DO NOT APPEAR ON THE COLOUR WHEEL AND ARE CONSIDERED NEUTRALS, YET WHEN TEAMED WITH COLOUR THEY MAKE THE COLOURS THEMSELVES APPEAR MORE VIBRANT.

FLAMBOYANT
FLORA

Colour inspiration... This wonderful red-breasted toucan, which I photographed on a teaching trip to Brazil, makes an excellent example of how colours in the natural world can inspire us. Its bold, contrasting plumage together with the green jungle backdrop make a striking cake. It may be because I love bright colours and colour contrast that I found this combination easy to use, but I expect it has more to do with the colours being adjacent to each other on the colour wheel and so naturally look good together.

ANALOGOUS COLOUR SCHEME

COLOURS OF THE NATURAL WORLD ARE OFTEN STRIKING AND PLEASING TO THE EYE, SO MAKE EXCELLENT COLOUR INSPIRATION FOR CAKES.

analogous colour scheme ...

THE NATIVE AUSTRALIAN BOTTLEBRUSH (CALLISTEMON) ADDS A DASH OF HOT RED.

A SUNLIT CALIFORNIAN POPPY MAKES A STRIKING COLOUR SPLASH.

THE SUN-SEEKING SUNFLOWER IN WARM, YELLOW TONES.

"Man needs colour to live; it's just as necessary an element as fire and water" — Fernand Leger

THIS DEEP ORANGE AND BLACK BUTTERFLY BRINGS DRAMA TO THE TROPICAL SCENE.

analogous colour scheme ...

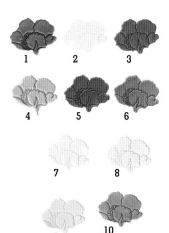

Mixing the colours

To recreate the colours I have used, add the following paste colours to white sugarpaste (rolled fondant) or use the sugarpaste I have suggested:

1 black: M&B black sugarpaste plus wisteria (SK)

2 ivory: M&B ivory sugarpaste

3 deep orange: nasturtium (SK) and red extra (SF)

4 light tangerine: tangerine/apricot (SF)

5 tangerine: tangerine (SF) plus a touch of sunflower (SK)

6 orange: nasturtium (SK)

7 yellow: cream (SF) and melon (SF)

8 deep yellow: sunflower (SK) and melon (SF)

9 lime green: vine (SK) plus a touch of gooseberry (SF)

10 olive green: gooseberry (SF) and paprika/flesh (SF)

You will need

materials

cakes: 1 round cake 25.5cm (10in), 4cm (1½in) high; 3 round cakes 15cm (6in), all 7.5cm (3in) high

sugarpaste (rolled fondant): 800g (1lb 12oz) deep orange; 180g (6oz) black; 2kg (4lb 8oz) ivory

modelling paste: 200g (7oz) black; 50g (2oz) each deep yellow, yellow, ivory, orange, lime green and olive green; 25g (1oz) each tangerine, light tangerine and deep orange

buttercream

piping gel

white vegetable fat (shortening)

sugar glue

tip FOR THE SHALLOW CAKE, BAKE A 20CM (8IN) RECIPE IN A 25.5CM (10IN) TIN (PAN).

equipment

cake boards: 1 round drum 33cm (13in); 1 round hardboard 25.5cm (10in); 3 round hardboards 15cm/12.5cm (6in/5in); 1 spare round drum 20cm (8in) or less

round polystyrene spacer 10cm (4in), 3cm (1¼in) high

9 or 10 dowels

15mm (⅝in) wide orange ribbon and non-toxic glue stick

cutters: large round pastry cutters, e.g. 7cm (2¾in) and 8cm (3¼in); pointed ovals (LC); flame (LC); rose leaf (FMM)

wild rose cutter/embosser set (PC)

moulds: blossom medium flower FL306 (FI); daisy set FL288 (FI); daisy centre stamp (JEM); heart set (AM)

sugar shaper

veiners: gardenia leaf (GI); small poppy leaf (GI); large poppy leaf (GI)

non-slip mat

waxed paper

... flamboyant flora

Preparation

Covering the board and spacer

1 Roll out the deep orange sugarpaste to a thickness of 5mm (⅕in), ideally using spacers, and use to cover the 33cm (13in) cake board.

2 Cover the polystyrene spacer with piping gel to help stick the sugarpaste. Roll out the black sugarpaste and use to cover the spacer, making sure that the bottom edge of the paste is neat (see Covering Cakes with Sugarpaste).

Stage one

Covering the shallow cake

1 Level the 25.5cm (10in) cake to a depth of 4cm (1½in) (see Levelling Cakes), then stick the cake onto the cake board of the same size using buttercream. Cover the whole cake in a thin layer of buttercream using a palette knife. Place a non-slip mat on top of the small cake drum and position the cake on top.

2 Roll out 800g (1lb 12oz) of the ivory sugarpaste between 5mm (⅕in) spacers, using white vegetable fat to prevent sticking. Lift up the paste, using a rolling pin for support, and place it over the cake. Using a smoother, smooth the paste in a circular motion to give a level surface, then use the palm of your hand to smooth the curved edge. Trim the sugarpaste flush with the underside of the board, taking care to keep the cut horizontal (**Fig A**). Set aside to dry.

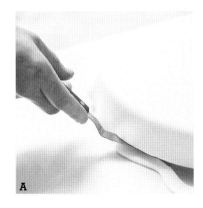

A

Covering the column cake

1 Level the three 15cm (6in) cakes each to a height of 7.5cm (3in). Place each on hardboard cake boards the same size or slightly smaller than the cakes themselves, securing them with buttercream.

2 Dowel the base and middle cakes (see Dowelling Cakes). Spread a thin layer of buttercream over the top of each cake and stack into the required shape. Check that the sides of your cake are completely vertical and adjust as necessary, then spread a thin layer of buttercream over the whole cake to stick the sugarpaste.

3 Knead the remaining ivory sugarpaste to warm it and then roll it out into a rectangular shape using 5mm (⅕in) spacers. Turn the paste over and cut it into a 33cm (13in) wide x 53cm (21in) long rectangle. Place the cake on its side on the paste so that the base is flush with one long edge. Roll up the cake in the paste, then trim the paste as necessary to create a neat straight join. Rub the join closed using the heat of your hand – it is easily disguised by the decoration.

4 Stand your cake upright on waxed paper and fold the sugarpaste over the top of the cake, cutting away the excess with scissors. Use a smoother to smooth the sides and top of the cake – the top will be covered with decoration, so don't worry about the joins.

Stage two

Assembling the cakes

1 Dowel the covered shallow cake and stack the cakes and the spacer centrally on the covered board (see Stacking Cakes).

2 Secure the orange ribbon to the cake board using a non-toxic glue stick.

Stage three

Adding the black floral decoration

1 To mark the position for the black decoration on the column cake, use the suggested circle cutters and a scriber and scribe semicircles around the cake. Scribe one about 2.5cm (1in) from the top of the cake and one on the opposite side 9cm (3½in) from the cake base, then join these two with three more on either side at differing heights to create a continuous sweep of curves. You don't need to be too exact, as the decoration will cover the lines; these are just to help with placement.

2 Knead the black modelling paste to warm it, adding a little white vegetable fat and cooled boiled water if the paste is a bit dry and crumbly; the paste should be pliable but firm.

3 Very thinly roll out some of the paste; the thickness is critical – too thick and the shapes will not cut out cleanly; too thin and the embossed

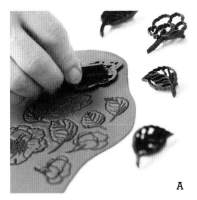

A

B

detail will not be as prominent. Press the cutters from the wild rose set firmly one by one into the paste (**Fig A**).

4 With the help of a scriber or similar tool, remove the paste from around the cut-outs (**Fig B**) and attach to the cake as shown in the main photo, overlapping to add texture and interest. Repeat as necessary.

tip LEAVE THE ROLLED-OUT PASTE ON YOUR WORK SURFACE TO FIRM UP SLIGHTLY BEFORE USING.

Creating the yellow multi-flowerheads

1 Knead a small amount of deep yellow modelling paste to warm it, then roll a ball about half the size of the blossom cavity on the medium flower mould. Place in the mould, ensuring that the sugar surface being placed in the mould is perfectly smooth; if there are small joins visible, they will probably be visible on your finished piece!

2 Push the paste into the mould firmly to spread it and to make sure that the deeper sections of the mould are filled. Stroke the paste up to the edges of the mould with your finger (**Fig A**). The paste in the mould should resemble a shallow cup.

3 Carefully flex the mould to release the flowers and encourage the back of the moulded flowers to flatten, in order to increase the contrast and visible detail in the flowers.

4 Using sugar glue, attach about five moulded shapes to the front and back of the cake to form two larger complete flowers, overlapping the moulded shapes as necessary (**Fig B**).

tip MOULDS ARE SIMPLE TO USE PROVIDED YOU SELECT THE RIGHT PASTE OF THE RIGHT CONSISTENCY FOR THE MOULD - USUALLY FIRM.

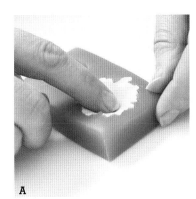

A

B

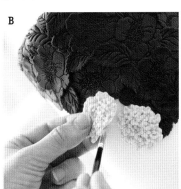

... flamboyant flora

Creating the feverfew (white daisies)

1 Knead a small amount of yellow modelling paste to warm it, then roll three small balls of paste smaller than the centre of the three largest daisies in the daisy mould set. Press the balls into the centre of the daisies.

2 Roll a ball of ivory modelling paste slightly larger than the mould cavity. Place in the mould, ensuring that the sugar surface being placed in the mould is perfectly smooth, and push in firmly.

3 Remove the excess paste with a palette knife so that the back of the mould is flat. Using a Dresden tool, make sure that each petal is properly defined by drawing the excess paste between petals into the centre. Repeat for all three daisies.

4 Carefully flex the mould to release the flowers. If the coloured centre has spread to the surrounding petals, add less paste to the centre next time.

5 Make about seven daisies. Cut each in half, then use your thumb and index finger to gently push the petals of each half together (**Fig A**).

6 Attach to the cake, overlapping the flowers for a natural feel (**Fig B**).

A

B

Creating the orange single daisy

1 Knead the tangerine modelling paste to warm it, adding a little white vegetable fat and cooled boiled water if the paste is a bit dry and crumbly; it should be pliable but firm.

2 Thinly roll the paste out, ideally using 1mm (1⁄32in) spacers. Use the flame cutters to cut out about 30 petals. Add these to the cake, arranging them in a two-layered radial pattern and giving movement to the petals (**Fig A**).

3 To create the flower centre, roll a ball of light tangerine modelling paste and press it firmly into the daisy centre stamp – use just enough paste to fill the mould without spilling out over the edges. The moulded paste

A

B

C

should come away cleanly from the mould attached to your finger (**Fig B**). Attach with sugar glue.

4 To make the tufts around the centre of the flower, soften some of the orange modelling paste so that it is really quite soft by adding a little white vegetable fat and cooled boiled water.

Place inside a sugar shaper with the small mesh disc. Push down the plunger and pump with the handle to squeeze out short lengths of paste (**Fig C**). Using a Dresden tool, remove a few tufts at a time and stick around the flower centre (if the paste doesn't come out easily, it isn't soft enough).

Creating the red heart flower

Using the 17mm (5⁄8in) wide heart from the heart mould set and the deep orange modelling paste, make about 18 moulded hearts and attach to the cake so that the tips of the hearts point towards a central point (**Fig A**).

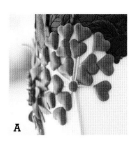

A

Creating the orange double dahlias

1 From thinly rolled-out orange modelling paste, cut out 26 petals 4.5cm (1¾in) long and 30 petals 2.5cm (1in) with the pointed oval cutters. Roll one end of each between thumb and index finger to shape (**Fig A**).

2 Attach 13 larger petals per flower to the cake in a radial pattern with sugar glue (**Fig B**). Add a layer of smaller petals on top. Then take six smaller petals, roll together at their base and add to the centre (**Fig C**).

A

B

C

Adding the stems

1 Create stems and stalks for each flower from softened green modelling pastes using the sugar shaper and all three round discs (**Fig A**). Paint the position of the stems on the cake with sugar glue, attach and cut to size with a craft knife.

2 To add fluffy texture to the stalks of the double dahlias, use the pointed end of a Dresden tool and indent and flick the surface of the soft paste. For the single orange daisy, using a pair of small scissors, carefully

snip into the extruded length of paste (**Fig B**), then attach to the cake.

A

B

Adding the leaves

1 Thinly roll out the green modelling pastes and use the rose leaf and pointed oval cutters of appropriate sizes to cut out leaves, then place on a foam pad. Use a ball tool to stroke around the edges of each leaf, pressing the tool half on the paste and half on the pad to soften the cut edge.

2 Place a leaf in an appropriate double-sided veiner, press down hard on the top of the veiner and then release and remove the veined leaf (**Fig A**). If the leaf looks a bit fleshy, the paste is too thick; if it has fallen apart in the veiner, the paste is probably too thin. Repeat for the remaining leaves.

3 Allow the leaves to firm up a little. Secure in place with sugar glue, giving movement to the paste for a

natural look (**Fig B**). For the orange single daisy, use the large poppy leaf veiner itself to cut out the leaf shape.

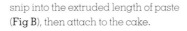

A

B

... flamboyant flora

Exotic posies

I love getting a little carried away when decorating cupcakes, and will do so whenever I have the time and it is appropriate. Here I wanted to include as many of the flowers from the main cake as possible to help illustrate the difference a background colour makes to the appearance of the same cupcake. I have chosen three backgrounds that are similar in colour to elements of the decoration and one that is not – can you see what happens, and which do you prefer?

1 Roll out the ivory sugarpaste to a thickness of 5mm (⅕in) using spacers. Cut circles of the paste large enough to snugly fit the top of your cupcakes and then position on top of your cupcakes.

2 Make moulded daisy and blossom flowers as for the main cake and attach to the cupcakes with sugar glue.

3 Create a small version of the orange double dahlia and add to the cupcakes.

4 Use the suggested cutters and veiners to cut out leaves from green modelling pastes and vein, then attach around the flowers.

tip FOR AN ALTERNATIVE LOOK, WHY NOT MAKE SINGLE FLOWER TYPE CUPCAKES AND DISPLAY THEM TOGETHER TO FORM A BOUQUET.

analogous colour scheme ...

WITH THE YELLOW BACKGROUND, THE YELLOW FLOWERS ALMOST VANISH, WHEREAS WITH THE DEEP RED BACKGROUND, THE ORANGE DAHLIA NO LONGER DOMINATES. ON THE BEIGE BACKGROUND, HOWEVER, THE LEAVES ARE NOT SO NOTICEABLE. IT IS ONLY ON THE NEUTRAL BROWN BACKGROUND THAT ALL THE ELEMENTS OF THE CUPCAKE ARE CLEARLY SEEN.

"Colours are brighter when the mind is open" – Adriana Alarcon

... flamboyant flora

EASTERN INFUSION

Colour inspiration...

I am always drawn to interesting colour combinations, so this Indian key ring caught my eye. I love red and purple together, but the two aqua blue flower buttons create an intriguing and unusual colour accent. I did consider creating a red teapot to closely mirror the colour proportions of the key ring, but red sugarpaste is not as attractive to eat as pale pink, so I confined the red to the decoration. I have, however, placed the teapot on a red stencilled board to lend it the same vibrancy as the red background of the key ring gives to its embellishments.

TWO AQUA BUTTONS INTRODUCE AN INTRIGUING COLOUR ACCENT TO THIS OPULENT BEJEWELLED KEY RING.

ANALOGOUS COLOUR SCHEME WITH COMPLEMENTARY ACCENT (THE AQUA BLUE)

MOSAIC TILES IN PRIMARY BLUES, REDS AND YELLOWS, MERLION WALK, SINGAPORE.

EXOTIC SPECKLED ORCHID IN RICH, OPULENT COLOURS.

POMEGRANATES IN A METALLIC BOWL, CAMPO DE' FIORI, ROME.

PINK WINTER BERRIES OF A MOUNTAIN ASH TREE STAND OUT AGAINST A WINTER SKY.

SRI MARIAMMAN TEMPLE IN SINGAPORE, A RIOT OF COLOUR YET BEAUTIFUL.

"Colour! What a deep and mysterious language, the language of dreams" – Paul Gaugin

analogous colour scheme with complementary accent ...

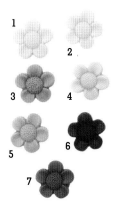

Mixing the colours

To recreate the colours I have used, add the following paste colours to white sugarpaste (rolled fondant) or use the sugarpaste I have suggested:

1 light pink: M&B ivory and pastel pink sugarpaste plus a touch of poinsettia (SK)
2 pale gold: autumn leaf (SF)
3 bronze: autumn leaf (SF) and chestnut (SF)
4 aqua blue: gentian (SK) and bluegrass (SK)

5 mid pink: rose (SK) and red extra (SF)
6 red: M&B red 2 sugarpaste plus red extra (SF)
7 purple: M&B amethyst sugarpaste plus rose (SK)

You will need

materials

cakes: 2 round cakes 12.5cm (5in), 7.5cm (3in) high

sugarpaste (rolled fondant): 650g (1lb 7oz) red; 1kg (2lb 4oz) light pink

modelling paste: 200g (7oz) bronze; 50g (2oz) each purple, red, light pink and mid pink; 25g (1oz) each pale gold and aqua blue

bronze edible lustre dust (SK)

buttercream

white vegetable fat (shortening)

sugar glue

confectioners' glaze

equipment

cake boards: 1 round drum 25.5cm (10in); 1 round hardboard 10cm or 9cm (4in or 3½in) (size depends on how much cake shrinks when it cools)

2 dowels

15mm (⅝in) wide purple ribbon and non-toxic glue stick

Victorian lace top (DS) stencil

sugar shaper

cutters: 2 hearts from Lindy's peacock set (LC); small teardrop set (LC); elegant heart (LC); large flat floral (LC); pointed oval (LC); Indian scrolls (LC)

piping tubes (tips): nos. 16 and 18 (PME)

flower from garden mould set (AM)

large soft dusting brush

waxed paper

... eastern infusion

Preparation

The cake board and teapot handle can be completed well in advance.

Covering and decorating the board

1 Roll out the red sugarpaste to a thickness of 5mm (⅛in), ideally using spacers, and use to cover your cake board. Trim the soft sugarpaste to size and immediately position the stencil centrally on top.

2 Place a smoother on top of the stencil and press down firmly so that the sugarpaste is forced up to the upper surface of the stencil (**Fig A**). Repeat the action, repositioning the smoother each time, so that the entire pattern of the stencil is embossed into the soft sugarpaste.

3 Using a finger or a paintbrush, smear a thin layer of white vegetable fat over the surface of the pattern (the paste that has been forced up through the stencil).

4 Dip a large dusting brush into the bronze edible lustre dust, knock off any excess and then liberally dust over the stencil, adding more dust as necessary (**Fig B**). Using your brush, remove any excess dust from the stencil, ensuring that as you lift the stencil no stray dust falls from the stencil to spoil the pattern beneath. Use the brush to burnish the dust to really make it shine (burnishing is not possible with all makes of edible dust).

5 Carefully peel the stencil away to reveal the pattern (**Fig C**).

6 Re-trim the board with a palette knife to give a neat finish. Attach the purple ribbon to the edge of the board with a non-toxic glue stick.

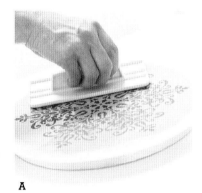

A

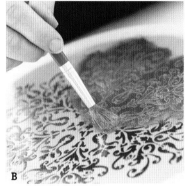

B

tip IT'S IMPORTANT TO USE A SOFT BRUSH; IF THE BRISTLES ARE TOO FIRM, THEY MAY LEAVE MARKS IN THE FINISH.

C

Making the teapot handle

1 Transfer the handle template to a piece of paper and cut a dowel to about 10cm (4in) in length.

2 Knead the bronze modelling paste to make it warm and flexible; if it's a little dry and crumbly, knead in a little white vegetable fat and cooled boiled water until soft and smooth.

3 Roll the paste into a 2cm (¾in) thick sausage. Cut across the sausage at right angles and insert the dowel along the length as shown on the template. Place the paste on the template and use your fingers to stroke the sausage into shape. Once the paste fits the template, cut across the end of the paste with a palette knife using the template as a guide.

4 Roll, smooth and cut another section of the sausage to fit the middle section of the template. Attach the two sections together at their join with sugar glue.

5 For the lower section of the handle, re-roll the modelling paste into a tapered sausage to fit the template, smooth to shape with your fingers and cut to size with a palette knife (**Fig A**). Attach to the first two sections with sugar glue.

6 Place the handle on a foam pad and leave to dry thoroughly – this could take a day or two depending on atmospheric conditions, so allow enough time.

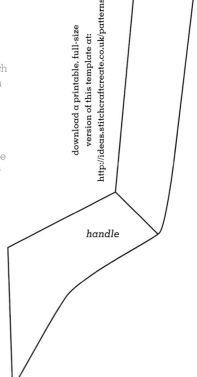

download a printable, full-size version of this template at:
http://ideas.stitchcraftcreate.co.uk/patterns

handle

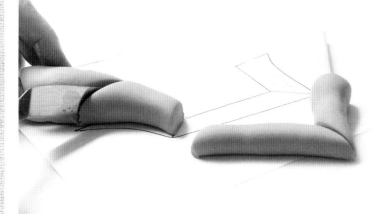

A

tip AN AIRING CUPBOARD IS AN EXCELLENT PLACE TO DRY SUGAR WORK.

... eastern infusion

Stage one

Carving and covering the cake

1 Level the cakes (see Levelling Cakes), split and fill with buttercream or jam etc., if required, then spread a thin layer of buttercream over the top of one cake and stack the other on top to create a column of cake 15cm (6in) tall.

2 Select the appropriate size of cake board, depending on how much your cake has shrunk when cooling – there must be a differential between the width of your board, i.e. the top of the cake, and the width of the bottom to allow for carving.

3 Place your board centrally on top of the cake column. Mark its position with a small knife, then take a sharp carving knife and carve from the edge of the board to the lower edge of the cake, to create a truncated tapered cone (**Fig A**).

4 Roll 100g (3½oz) of the pink sugarpaste into a ball, then flatten and place on top of your cake board. Stroke the paste into a shallow even dome with your hand.

5 Spread a thin layer of buttercream over the side and top of the cake to stick the sugarpaste. Place the small covered board on top of the cake.

6 Knead the remaining pink sugarpaste and then roll it out between 5mm (⅕in) spacers. Turn the paste over and cut it into a rectangle about 20cm (8in) wide x 48cm (19in) long. Place the cake on the paste and roll up in the paste (**Fig B**). Note that as the cake is tapered it will roll in a slight curve, so make an allowance for this when positioning the cake on the paste.

tip IT'S OFTEN EASIER TO ROLL THE SUGARPASTE INTO A SAUSAGE THE CORRECT LENGTH BEFORE ROLLING IT FLAT WITH A ROLLING PIN.

7 Trim the paste as necessary to create a neat join – it will be covered by decoration, so the finish isn't too important, but try to keep it as vertical as possible.

8 Trim the paste flush with the base of the cake using a palette knife (**Fig C**). Carefully stand the cake upright on waxed paper. At the top of the cake, carefully cut away the excess paste with scissors (**Fig D**). Smooth the sides with a smoother, then set aside to dry.

A

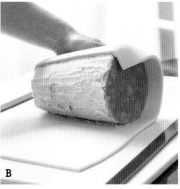

B

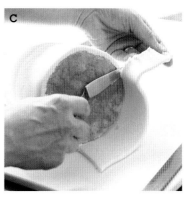

C

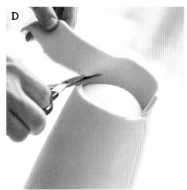

D

analogous colour scheme with complementary accent ...

Stage two

Adding the spout and handle

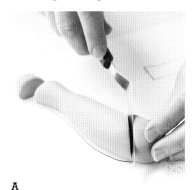

A

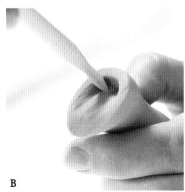

B

1 Warm the remaining bronze modelling paste, roll into a thick tapered sausage and shape to fit the spout template. Place the paste on the template and use a palette knife to cut across the paste at either end to form the spout and base (**Fig A**).

2 Push a sugar glue-covered dowel up through the spout as shown on the template. Shape the tip of the spout by pinching the paste between your fingers, then use a Dresden tool to indent the pouring hole (**Fig B**).

3 On the opposite side of the cake to the sugarpaste join, insert the dowel of the spout into the cake 6cm (2⅜in) up from the base of the cake, at the same angle as shown on the template. Use sugar glue to help attach the modelling paste of the spout to the sugarpaste of the cake. Support in place with foam if necessary.

4 Place a little sugar glue on either end of the handle and insert the other dowel over the paste join, on the opposite side of the cake to the spout, 1.5cm (⅝in) below the top rim of the cake, until both sections of the handle sit flush with the sides of the cake.

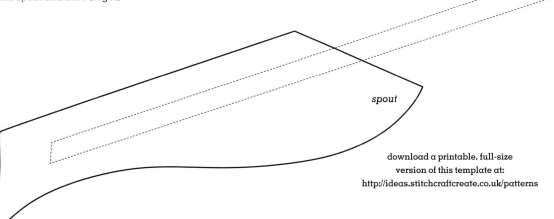

spout

download a printable, full-size
version of this template at:
http://ideas.stitchcraftcreate.co.uk/patterns

Adding the bronze trim

1 Using a paintbrush, paint a thin line of sugar glue around the base of the cake, handle and spout.

2 Soften some of the bronze modelling paste so that it is really quite soft by adding a little white vegetable fat and cooled boiled water. Place inside a sugar shaper with the medium round disc. Push down the plunger and pump with the handle

to squeeze out a length of paste, then place around the base of the cake (**Fig A**) – if the paste doesn't come out easily, it isn't soft enough.

3 Replace the medium round disc with the small disc and squeeze out two lengths of paste. Allow to firm up a little before placing them around the base of the handle and spout, trimming to fit as necessary.

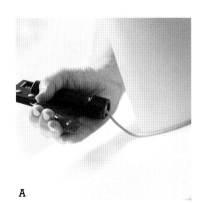

A

... eastern infusion

Stage three

Adding shine

Once the paste of the spout and bronze decoration has had time to dry, mix the bronze edible lustre dust with confectioners' glaze and use to paint over all the dried bronze modelling paste to give the teapot a touch of opulence.

Adding the decoration

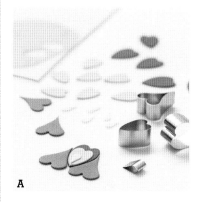

A

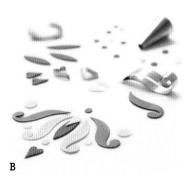

B

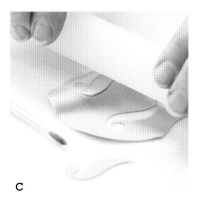

C

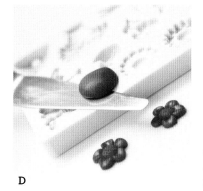

D

1 For the decoration around the base of the teapot, separately roll out the purple, red, pink and gold modelling pastes, ideally between 1mm (1⁄32in) spacers. Use the suggested cutters to cut out about 23 of each shape (**Fig A**). Attach in place around the base of the cake with sugar glue.

tip USE A STAY FRESH MAT TO PREVENT YOUR ROLLED-OUT PASTE FROM DRYING OUT.

2 To make the teapot rim, soften some light pink modelling paste and place inside the sugar shaper with the large round disc. Push down the plunger and squeeze out a length of paste, then place over the raw top edge of the sugarpaste sides of the teapot and secure with sugar glue. Replace the disc with the smallest round and squeeze out two lengths of

paste. Allow the lengths to firm up a little while you paint sugar glue over the joins between the side of the cake and rim and the rim and lid. Once the lengths are firm enough to handle, stick in place and cut to size.

3 For the pattern just below the rim, separately roll out the purple, red, pink, aqua blue and gold modelling pastes, ideally between 1mm (1⁄32in) spacers. Use the suggested cutters to cut out enough shapes for four pattern repeats (**Fig B**). When using the Indian scroll cutters, I often find it is easier to place the paste over the cutter (**Fig C**) and roll over it with a rolling pin before releasing the paste with a paintbrush. For the circles, use the nos. 16 and 18 piping tubes as cutters.

4 Create six small red moulded flowers by pushing a small ball of red modelling paste into the suggested mould and cutting the excess away with a palette knife (**Fig D**) before flexing the mould to release the flower. Attach all the prepared pieces in place with sugar glue.

5 To create the central motifs, cut out three large flat florals from thinly rolled-out aqua blue modelling paste, then use the teardrop cutter from the set to remove small triangles of paste from each petal (**Fig E**). Separate each petal with a craft knife (**Fig F**). Take six petals for each motif and attach them centrally to each side of the teapot so that all the petals touch. Add a purple centre to each motif, using the larger end of a piping tube as a cutter, then decorate with small gold teardrops and six red circles cut out using the no. 16 tube.

6 To disguise the vertical join in the sugarpaste between the ends of the handle, cut circles of differing sizes from light pink modelling paste and use to create a self-pattern.

7 For the lid, roll a 2.7cm (1in) ball of pink modelling paste and place on top of the pot. Add purple trim around the ball using the sugar shaper and the medium round disc. Decorate around this with seven red elegant hearts and circles of pink (no. 18 tube) and blue (no. 16 tube).

8 Once you are happy with the decoration, transfer the cake to its prepared decorated board.

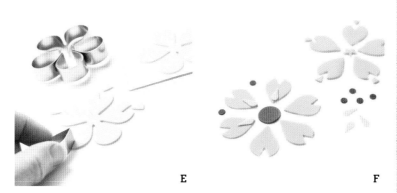

E **F**

... eastern infusion

mug cookies and cutter (LC)

70g (2½in) sugarpaste (rolled fondant) per cookie, colours as for the main cake

bronze edible lustre dust (SK)

Victorian lace top stencil (DS)

large soft dusting brush

white vegetable fat (shortening)

piping gel

edible spray glaze

Magical mugs

For these simple yet striking mug cookies, I have chosen to illustrate how colours mutually influence each other by showing how the bronze stencilled pattern is affected by the background colour of the sugarpaste. Complementary colours are known to make each other appear brighter and balanced, which is why the aqua-coloured cookie looks one of the most appealing of my examples. A slight variation in the tint of a colour can make a noticeable impact on the overall appearance, as demonstrated in the two pink cookies.

1 Roll out one of the sugarpaste colours to a thickness of 5mm (⅛in), ideally using spacers. Place the stencil on top of the sugarpaste. Place a smoother on top of the stencil and then press down firmly so that the sugarpaste is forced up to the upper surface of the stencil.

2 Smear a thin layer of white vegetable fat over the surface of the pattern (the paste that has been forced up through the stencil).

3 Dip a large soft dusting brush into the lustre dust, knock off any excess and then liberally dust over the stencil, adding more dust as necessary.

4 Carefully lift the stencil away from the paste to reveal the pattern.

5 Using the cookie cutter, select the section of the pattern that looks appealing and cut out some mug shapes. Remove the excess paste from around the shapes and the area of the handle to give a more or less symmetrical shape. Using a cranked-handled palette knife and a quick swiping action so as not to distort the shape, position the knife under the sugarpaste shape.

6 Carefully lift the stencilled paste shape and position it on a cookie that has been partly covered with piping gel – don't add gel to the handle area. Remove the palette knife and if necessary, using a clean finger, press the paste so that it is all in contact with the cookie. If you need to do this more than once, ensure that your fingers are clean, to avoid spoiling the pattern.

7 Roll a sausage of paste and use to make a handle.

8 Repeat as required using the other sugarpaste colours.

9 Once complete, leave to dry and then spray each cookie with edible spray glaze to fix the dust – this prevents the dust from smudging, allowing the cookies to be stacked and placed in cookie bags without spoiling the stencilled pattern.

"Life without colour is unimaginable; fortunately most of us don't have to try" – Sheila Timmins

THE PATTERN ON THE MID PINK COOKIE SEEMS TO BLEND IN AND DIMINISH ON ITS BACKGROUND, WHEREAS IT IS MUCH MORE DISTINCTIVE AND PROMINENT ON THE PALE PINK COOKIE. ANALOGOUS COLOUR SCHEMES - THOSE THAT USE COLOURS ADJACENT TO EACH OTHER ON THE COLOUR WHEEL - ARE EASY TO USE AND VERY EFFECTIVE, AS IN THE RED AND BRONZE COOKIE, WHICH CERTAINLY STANDS OUT FROM THE CROWD.

... eastern infusion

PERFUME
PERFECTION

Colour inspiration...

I must be honest, I'm not a great fan of pale and pastel colours. However, for this art nouveau-styled perfume bottle cake I think the subtle shade of pale pink I have chosen is perfect. Lisianthus are delicate trumpet-shaped flowers that often change colour as they mature. Initially I had planned to incorporate the deeper pink of the mature flower as well, but as the cake developed I decided that the understated pale pink of the bud was more appropriate.

THE PASTEL PINK AND UNFURLING FORM OF THE LISIANTHUS FLOWER MAKE THE BASIS OF A VERY FEMININE CAKE DESIGN.

MONOCHROMATIC COLOUR SCHEME

APPLE BLOSSOM HAS EXQUISITE GRADATIONS OF DELICATE PINK.

A MAJESTIC CHANDELIER REFLECTS THE COLOUR OF THE ROOM IN A SOFT DIFFUSION OF PINK.

THIS JAPANESE ANEMONE DISPLAYS BEAUTIFUL TINTS OF PINK.

"Colour is the language of the poets. It is astonishingly lovely. To speak it is a privilege" – Keith Crown

THE SOFT PINK PETALS OF THE LISIANTHUS BUD UNFURL SO ARTISTICALLY.

THE EARLY SUMMER BLOOMS OF THIS ESCALLONIA ARE ANOTHER STUDY IN SUBTLE PINKS.

BEAUTIFUL PINK VELVET STAR-SHAPED FLOWERS OF A HOYA VINE.

Mixing the colour

To recreate the colour I have used, add the following paste colours to white sugarpaste (rolled fondant):

pale dusky pink: dusky pink (SF) and cream (SF)

You will need

materials

10cm (4in) ball cake

1 quantity royal icing, plus extra icing (confectioners') sugar to thicken if needed

50g (2oz) pale dusky pink flower (petal/gum) paste

350g (12oz) pale dusky pink sugarpaste (rolled fondant)

100g (3½oz) pale dusky pink modelling paste

edible dusts: superwhite (SF); rose (SK); snowflake lustre (SK)

buttercream

sugar glue

white vegetable fat (shortening)

equipment

round mirror cake board 20cm (8in)

vintage botanical stencil (LC)

lisianthus petal cutter (LC)

random veining tool (HP)

sugar shaper

18-gauge white floristry wire

small posy pick

no. 2 piping tube (tip) (PME)

soft dusting brush

waxed paper

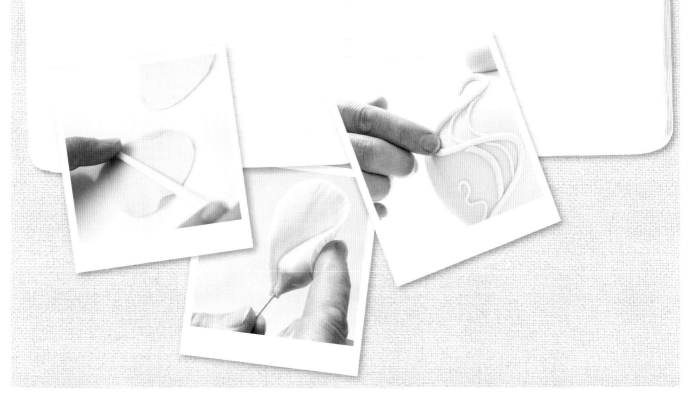

95

Preparation

Stencilling the mirror board

1 Colour the royal icing by firstly adding a little superwhite edible dust (this stops the dried icing looking too opaque), then the pink and cream paste colours to make a pale warm pink. Adjust the consistency if necessary – the icing should be firm enough not to seep under the stencil or flood the pattern once the stencil is removed, but not too firm that it is difficult to spread smoothly – adding icing (confectioners') sugar to thicken it or cooled boiled water to soften it.

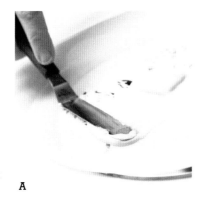

A

B

2 Position the stencil slightly off-centre on the mirror board. Place the coloured icing in the centre of the stencil so that the weight of the icing acts as an anchor, preventing the stencil from moving. Using a cranked-handled palette knife, carefully begin spreading the icing out from the centre with long radial strokes that go right to the edge of the stencil (**Fig A**). Remove any remaining icing on the knife at the end of each stroke.

3 Once the stencil is completely covered, work towards achieving an even thickness of icing but removing any excess with more careful strokes. Once you are happy with the finish, carefully peel the stencil away (**Fig B**).

tip TO CLEAN THE STENCIL, PLACE IN A BOWL OF WATER TO DISSOLVE THE ROYAL ICING AND THEN PAT DRY.

A

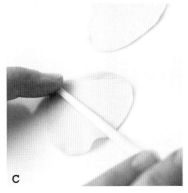

B

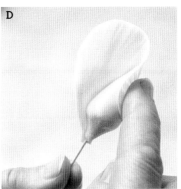

C

D

E

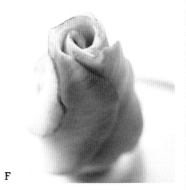

F

Creating the bud stopper

1 Roll a 2cm (¾in) ball of flower paste in your hand, then place the edge of the top hand next to the ball and roll the ball backwards and forwards until it turns into a cone (**Fig A**).

2 Cut a white wire into thirds. Carefully place the end of a piece of wire in a naked flame such as a gas cooker burner or a candle until it is red hot, then quickly insert it into the base of the flower paste cone (the heat of the wire melts the sugar and sets the cone securely on the wire). Pinch the paste down the stem and roll between your fingers to thin and shape. Leave to dry completely.

3 Very thinly roll out some of the flower paste. Use the largest cutter from the lisianthus set to cut out five petals. Turn the petals over and place on a foam pad (if you don't have a foam pad, use the palm of your hand). Use a ball tool to stroke around the edges of the each petal, pressing the tool half on the petal and half on the pad to soften the cut edge and to frill the edges slightly (**Fig B**).

4 Turn the petals back over and add texture by rolling over each with a random veining tool, placing the point of the tool at the base of the petals and pressing down gently while rolling the tool in a radial movement (**Fig C**).

tip YOU CAN CREATE THE BUD STOPPER FROM MODELLING PASTE INSTEAD, BUT MORE DELICATE PETALS ARE ACHIEVABLE WHEN USING FLOWER PASTE.

5 Cover the dried flower paste cone with sugar glue. Place a textured petal on the cone so that the base of the cone rests on the base of the petal. Stick half of the petal vertically to the cone (**Fig D**) and wrap it fairly tightly around the cone to start to create an anti-clockwise spiral, making sure that the centre of the cone is not visible.

6 Paint the section of petal stuck to the cone with sugar glue and place on top of the second petal as shown (**Fig E**), then wrap the second petal over the first.

7 Add the remaining three petals in the same way, tucking the last petal under. Adjust the position of the petals as necessary to create a tight spiral (**Fig F**).

8 Carefully dust the edges of the petals with the rose dust. If desired, set the dust by passing the flower briefly through steam. Place to one side.

... perfume perfection

Stage one

Covering the cake

1 Level the two cake halves (see Using a Ball Tin/Levelling Cakes) and then stick them together with buttercream (or chocolate ganache) so that the cake makes a perfect sphere. Place the cake on waxed paper and cover with buttercream.

2 Roll out the sugarpaste to a thickness of 5mm (⅕in), ideally using spacers, into a circle the same diameter as the circumference of your cake. Place the paste over the ball cake (**Fig A**), ease it around the base of the cake and pull up the excess to form two pleats (**Fig B**).

3 Cut the pleats away with scissors (**Fig C**) and smooth the joins closed – they should disappear fairly readily with the heat of your hand. Trim any excess paste away from the base of the cake. Using a smoother followed by your hand, smooth the surface of the cake with vertical strokes (**Fig D**). It is worth spending time doing this; the paste will not dry out if you continually work it. Set the cake aside to dry.

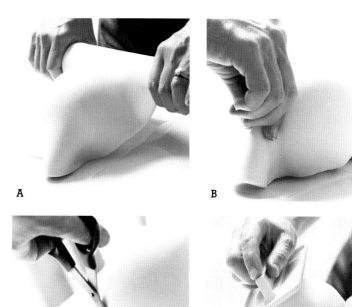

A B
C D

tip PLAN AHEAD WHERE TO PLACE YOUR PLEATS SO THAT THEY CAN EASILY BE COVERED WITH DECORATION.

Stage two

Adding the art nouveau decorations

1 Roll a 2.5cm (1in) ball of sugarpaste, position this on top of the covered cake and flatten the top with a smoother.

2 Add a little white vegetable fat to the modelling paste to stop it getting too sticky, then dunk the paste into a container of cooled boiled water and knead to incorporate. Repeat until the paste feels soft and stretchy like chewed chewing gum.

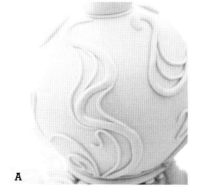

A

B

3 Insert the softened paste into the barrel of a sugar shaper, then add the large round disc and reassemble the tool. Push the plunger down to expel the air and pump the handle to build up pressure until it 'bites'. The paste should squeeze out easily and smoothly; if it doesn't, the consistency is probably incorrect, so remove the paste and add some more fat/water.

4 Wrap the resulting length of paste around the base of the cake and trim to fit with a craft knife.

5 Replace the disc in the shaper with the medium round disc and squeeze out a few lengths onto your work surface. Change the disc to the small round disc and squeeze out additional lengths, then allow them all to firm up a little. In the meantime, take a paintbrush and dip it into sugar glue, then referring to the finished cake photos (**Fig A** shows the back of the cake), start to paint freehand one or two of the sections of the pattern onto the cake (**Fig B**).

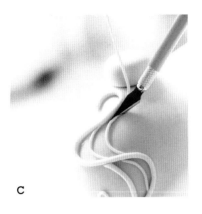

C

tip THE SMALLER THE HOLE IN THE DISC USED IN THE SUGAR SHAPER, THE SOFTER THE PASTE WILL NEED TO BE.

6 Pick up the lengths and place onto the glued pattern, trimming to fit as necessary with a craft knife (**Fig C**).

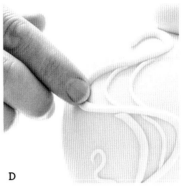

D

7 Once the sections you are working on are complete, flatten parts of the soft paste loops with your finger to give the design a more art nouveau feel (**Fig D**).

The finishing touches

1 Insert a small posy pick into the centre of the stopper and place the prepared lisianthus bud in position. Add a ring of paste around the base of the flower to neaten the appearance by using the sugar shaper and the medium round disc.

2 Replace the disc in the sugar shaper with the no. 2 piping tube and squeeze out two lengths – your paste needs to be very soft to do this. Place one length around the base of the cake to neaten the join between the trim and the cake, and another around the base of the stopper.

3 Using a soft dusting brush, dust the entire cake with the snowflake lustre dust to give the cake an attractive subtle shine.

4 Finally, transfer the decorated cake to the prepared decorated mirror board.

... perfume perfection

You will need

ankle boot cookies and cutter (LC)

70g (2½oz) sugarpaste (rolled fondant) per cookie, colour as for the main cake

royal icing, coloured as for the main cake

modelling paste, coloured as for the main cake

snowflake edible lustre dust (SK)

vintage botanical stencil (LC)

sugar shaper

soft dusting brush

piping gel

Fairytale footwear

I always love creating edible shoes, as there is something very attractive and desirable about them! Here I have taken elements and the colour from the main cake and created a rather glitzy ankle boot. However, how the colours of this cookie bootie both appear and feel is very dependent on the background colour on which it is displayed. I have chosen both some subtle pastel and strong colour shades to highlight the difference.

1 Roll out some sugarpaste to a thickness of 5mm (⅛in), ideally using spacers. Cut out a shape using the cookie cutter, but leave the excess paste in place, as this helps to support the stencil, allowing it to lie flat. Position the pattern of the stencil on the cut-out boot as desired. Using a palette knife, carefully spread the coloured royal icing over the relevant section of the stencil. Use one or two strokes, working from one side of the stencil to another.

tip DON'T AT ANY POINT LIFT THE PALETTE KNIFE, AS THIS MAY CAUSE THE STENCIL TO ALSO LIFT AND SMUDGE THE PATTERN.

2 Once the icing is of an even thickness, carefully remove the stencil. Remove all the excess sugarpaste from around the stencilled shape. Paint piping gel over the cookie to act as glue.

3 Using a clean palette knife and a quick swiping action so as not to distort the shape, position the palette knife under the sugarpaste shape before carefully lifting it and placing on top of the cookie.

4 Use a cutting wheel to mark the heel of the boot.

5 Add some art nouveau-style decoration as for the main cake using the sugar shaper and the small round disc.

6 Dust the cookie with the lustre dust – it will stick readily to the soft sugarpaste and decoration but not the hardened royal icing, creating an interesting effect.

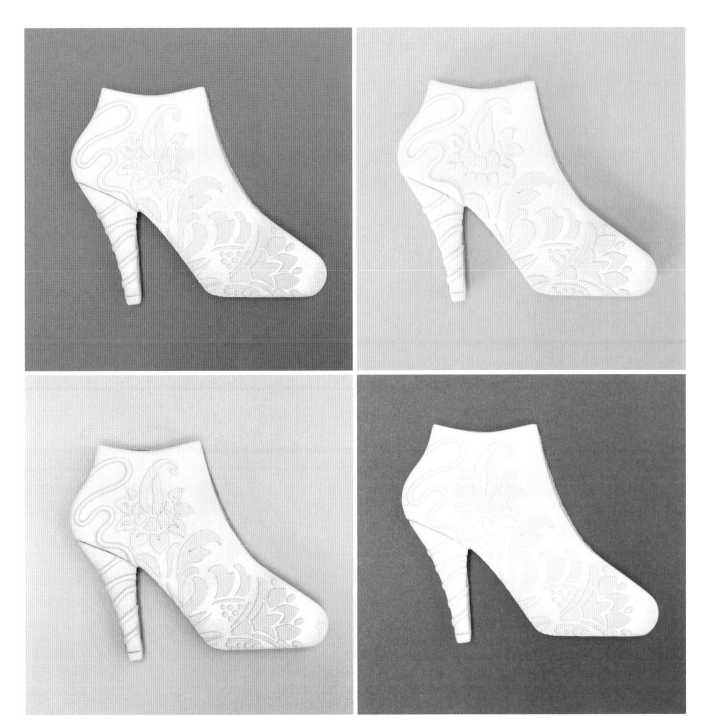

WHEN THE COOKIE IS DISPLAYED ON A PALER BACKGROUND, THE DETAIL AND TEXTURE OF THE BOOT IS NOTICEABLE AT FIRST GLANCE, BUT AS SOON AS THE COOKIE IS PLACED ON A DARKER, STRONGER BACKGROUND, IT IS THE OVERALL SHAPE THAT DOMINATES RATHER THAN ANY DETAIL.

"Colour is determined by amount, application and placement" – Charles Emerson

... perfume perfection

PATCHWORK *owl*

Colour inspiration...

I love colours and I love using them on cakes, so for this adorable patchwork-style owl design I decided that it was highly appropriate to use the whole spectrum of colours – well, 12 to be exact. My colour reference for this project was my daughter's colourful ring binder with its pretty pinks and purples, its interesting greens and striking oranges. I have taken these colours and mixed, matched and balanced them to illustrate that cakes can certainly be colourful and that a polychromatic colour scheme using colours from right around the colour wheel can be successful.

BOLD, FUN, COLOURFUL GRAPHICS FOUND ON EVERYDAY ITEMS LIKE THIS RING BINDER CAN OFFER CREATIVE COLOUR SCHEME IDEAS.

Unique Graphics ring binder © Staples www.staples.co.uk

POLYCHROMATIC COLOUR SCHEME

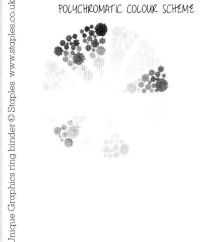

MOUTHWATERING RASPBERRY FILLING TOPPED BY THE DEEP PURPLE OF A BLACKBERRY.

COLOURFUL CHRISTMAS BAUBLES CREATE A PERFECT POLYCHROMATIC COLOUR SCHEME.

BEAUTIFUL GREEN STAINED GLASS IN THE ROYAL ARCADE, NORWICH.

A FABULOUS MEDLEY OF FESTIVAL LANTERNS, CHINATOWN, SINGAPORE.

"Colours must fit together as pieces in a puzzle or cogs in a wheel" – Hans Hofmann

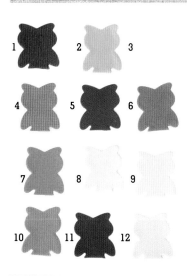

Mixing the colours

To recreate the colours I have used, add the following paste colours to white sugarpaste (rolled fondant) or use the sugarpaste I have suggested:

1 very deep pink: pink (SF)
2 pale pink: pink (SF)
3 ivory: M&B ivory sugarpaste
4 mid pink: rose (SK)
5 dark grey: eucalyptus (SF) plus a touch of black extra (SF)
6 lavender: plum (SK) and red extra (SF)
7 orange: berberis (SK) plus a touch of marigold (SK)
8 pale blue: bluegrass (SK) and wisteria (SK)

9 lime green: bitter lemon/lime (SF) plus a touch of gooseberry (SF)
10 olive green: gooseberry (SF)
11 purple: plum (SK) plus a touch of red extra (SF)
12 pale green: gentian (SK) and party green (SF)

You will need

materials

25.5cm (10in) square cake, 7.5cm (3in) high

sugarpaste (rolled fondant): 800g (1lb 12oz) lime green; 500g (1lb 2oz) pale green; 700g (1lb 9oz) ivory; 400g (14oz) purple

modelling paste: 75g (2¾oz) each mid pink, lavender and pale green; 50g (2oz) each pale pink, purple, olive green and pale blue; 25g (1oz) each very deep pink, dark grey, ivory and lime green; 100g (3½oz) orange

buttercream

sugar glue

equipment

round cake drum (board) 35.5cm (14in)

15mm (⅝in) wide purple ribbon and non-toxic glue stick

stencils: daisy and forget-me-not (C547) (DS); daisy lattice (C378) (DS); contemporary wave cake top (LC); retro circle (LC); peony (LC)

cutters: strawberry and flower from cupcake set (PC); large flat floral (LC); Chinese scroll set (LC); for the eyes: 10cm (4in), 9cm (3½in), 4.3cm (1¾in), 3cm (1⅛in) and 2.3cm (1in) circle (I used pastry cutters); 8.5cm (3⅜in) large sunflower plunger (PME); 6.5cm (2½in) rose (FMM)

piping tubes (tips): nos. 1, 4, 16, 17 and 18 (PME)

embossers: flower embossing stamps set 1 (FMM); butterflies – set 18 (HP); bee – set 7 (HP); lace – set 19 (HP); flower – small floral set 1 (HP); cherries from fruit & cooking utensils set (PC)

perfect pearls 8mm (⅚in) mould

waxed paper

... patchwork owl

Preparation

Covering and decorating the board

1 Roll out the lime green sugarpaste to a thickness of 5mm (⅛in), ideally using spacers, and use to cover your cake board. Trim the soft sugarpaste to size and immediately position the daisy and forget-me-not stencil on the board so that the flowers lie over the edge of the board.

2 Place a smoother on top of the stencil and press down firmly so that the sugarpaste is forced up to the

upper surface of the stencil (**Fig A**). Repeat, repositioning the smoother so that the entire pattern of the stencil is embossed into the soft sugarpaste. Move the stencil and repeat until the board is ringed with self-coloured flowers. Re-trim the board as required to give a neat finish.

3 Set aside to dry. Once dry, add the purple ribbon to the board using a non-toxic glue stick.

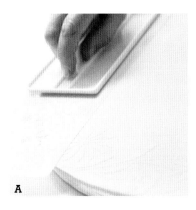

A

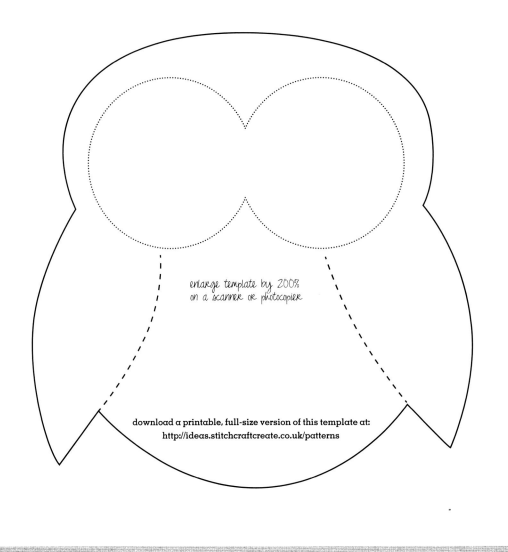

enlarge template by 200% on a scanner or photocopier

download a printable, full-size version of this template at:
http://ideas.stitchcraftcreate.co.uk/patterns

Stage one

Carving the cake

1 Enlarge the owl template at 200% to give the owl a height and width of 24cm (9½in) and then cut out from waxed paper.

2 Level the cake (see Levelling Cakes), then place the template on top, securing it with cocktail sticks (toothpicks). Using a sharp carving knife, cut vertically through the cake around the template edge (**Fig A**).

3 Insert cocktail sticks along the inner edges of the wing lines (**Fig B**). Mark the meeting points of the two eyes with cocktail sticks, then carefully lift the template off the cake leaving the cocktail sticks in place.

4 Carefully push the 9cm (3½in) circle cutter twice into the cake to a depth of 1.5cm (⅝in) to mark the position of both eyes (**Fig C**).

5 Take a sharp carving knife and dome the tummy area by cutting from the centre down to the cocktail sticks marking the wings and the marked eyes. Round the lower edge to give a smooth curve, referring to the step photo (**Fig D**) and finished cake.

6 Remove all the cocktail sticks and carefully shape each wing as shown (**Fig E**). Next curve the top of the head, the area above and to the side of the owl's eyes.

7 Once you are happy with the overall shape of the cake, insert the point of a small sharp knife from the outer edge of the eye into the centre and carefully cut around the eye to remove a shallow cone shape. Repeat for the second eye (**Fig F**).

enlarge template at 200% on a scanner or photocopier

download a printable, full-size version of this template at: http://ideas.stitchcraftcreate.co.uk/patterns

A

B

C

D

E

F

... patchwork owl

Covering the cake

1 Place the cake on waxed paper and spread a thin layer of buttercream over just the tummy area to stick the sugarpaste.

2 Knead the pale green sugarpaste to warm and roll out, ideally between 5mm (⅕in) spacers. Place the centre of the daisy lattice stencil on one corner of the paste. Using a smoother, press down firmly to force the soft sugarpaste up to the upper surface of the stencil. Pick up the paste and place on the buttercream so that the daisy pattern is positioned directly under the owl's right eye. Ease in the paste's fullness around the base and cut away the excess paste adjacent to the wings and eye with a palette knife (**Fig A**). Place a smoother against the base of the cake, press down to create a neat cutting line and remove the excess with a palette knife.

3 Cover one wing with buttercream. Roll out some of the ivory sugarpaste and cut one edge straight. Pick up the paste and place over the

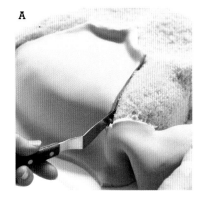

A

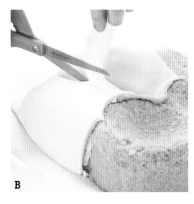

B

wing so that the straight edge rests on the waxed paper on the outside base of the wing. Using a pair of scissors, roughly remove the excess paste that overlaps the pale green sugarpaste (**Fig B**), then cut to size using a craft knife so that the sugarpaste colours abut. Repeat for the second wing.

4 Cover the top of the head with rolled-out purple sugarpaste randomly embossed with the flower from the cupcake set. Ease in the fullness and trim. Use the 9cm (3½in) circle cutter to remove the purple

sugarpaste from the eye area and replace it with a slightly larger circle – the size will depend on how deeply you have carved the eye socket; I used a 10cm (4in) cutter.

Stage two

The pink heart

1 Enlarge the heart template at 200% and then cut out from waxed paper or similar.

2 Thinly roll out the mid pink modelling paste, ideally using 1mm (¹⁄₃₂in) spacers, slightly larger than the heart. Place the contemporary wave stencil on top. Use a smoother to press down so that the paste is forced up to the upper surface of the stencil. Repeat, repositioning the smoother so that the entire pattern is embossed. Cover with a stay fresh mat to prevent the paste drying out.

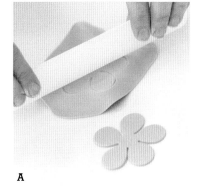

A

3 Thinly roll out the pale pink modelling paste, place over the large flat floral cutter and roll over the paste with a rolling pin (**Fig A**), then rub a finger around the edge of the cutter to achieve a clean cut. Turn the cutter over and remove the shape with the help of a paintbrush. Repeat to make three. Using the trimmings, cut out a selection of circles using the nos. 16 and 18 piping tubes.

4 Position the flat florals and small circles on the textured mid pink paste, using the heart template to aid placement. Use the teardrop cutter from the flat floral set to remove sections from each flower to create a large broderie anglaise look (**Fig B**). Then remove the centres of each circle using the nos. 17 and 4 piping tubes (**Fig C**).

5 Place the heart template on top of the broderie anglaise pattern and use a craft knife to cut out the pink heart (**Fig D**). Attach to the centre of the owl's front as shown in the photo of the finished cake.

B

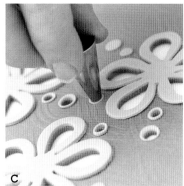

C

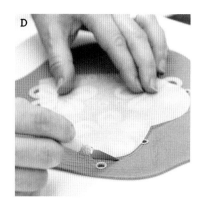

D

The owl's sides

1 For the purple polka dot patchwork section, thinly roll out the purple modelling paste, ideally between 1mm (1/32in) spacers so that it is the same thickness as the heart. Place the heart template on one side of the paste and use a craft knife to cut away this part of the heart outline. Position the paste so that it abuts the heart on the cake. Cut away the excess paste from the wings and base carefully with the craft knife and make a vertical cut at the base of the heart.

2 Remove circles using the no. 18 piping tube and replace with olive green ones.

3 For the strawberry patchwork, thinly roll out the lavender paste and emboss with the strawberry cutter. Cut the paste as for the other side and position and trim as before. Very thinly roll out some deep pink, dark grey and ivory modelling pastes and cut out the relevant strawberry parts and some ivory hearts. Attach in place on the cake and emboss each heart with a small flower embosser.

... patchwork owl

The wings

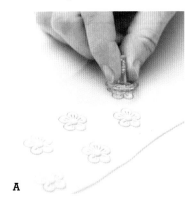

A

B

C

1 Starting on the owl's left-hand inner wing sections, thinly roll out some pale green modelling paste and use one of the suggested stencils to add texture. Cut one edge of the paste straight and position this on the owl's wing so that it neatly abuts the decorated tummy and sides of the owl. Cut away the paste along the top of the wing with a craft knife so that it forms a neat curved shape.

2 For the top blue section of the wing, thinly roll out the pale blue modelling paste into a strip and randomly emboss with a flower embosser (**Fig A**), leaving space between the flowers. Cut one edge straight and place on the cake against the pale green inner wing section. Using a craft knife, cut the paste from the tip of the wing up to the eye to create a pointed feather shape, as seen on the finished cake. Use the five-petal flower cutter from the flat floral set to cut out flowers from the deep pink modelling paste and attach to the cake in the spaces between the embossed flowers. Use the no. 16 piping tube to remove the centre of each dark pink flower to reveal the ivory sugarpaste below. Emboss around each cut-out circle with the tip of a no. 1 tube.

3 Emboss some mid pink modelling paste with butterflies and add to the cake as in the previous step, again cutting the paste into a feather shape on the cake itself.

4 Finish off the wing by adding an olive green section and then cutting and replacing circles with a no. 17 piping tube (**Fig B**).

5 Decorate the second wing in the same way using the suggested pastes, cutters, embossers and stencils or ones from your own tool box (**Fig C**).

A

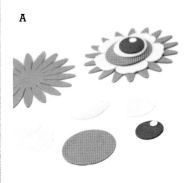

The eyes

1 Thinly roll out all the modelling paste colours needed to create the eyes and use the appropriate cutters to cut out two of each shape (**Fig A**).

2 Attach the large lavender sunflowers centrally in the eye sockets, ensuring that the petals are evenly spaced. Add the pale blue rose on top.

3 Roll a 10g (¼oz) ball of ivory sugarpaste for each eye, flatten it slightly and add to the centre of the hollow to give the eyeball a domed shape. Then attach the cut circles in place as shown (**Fig A**). Experiment with the position of the light spot, as this can really enhance your owl's appearance and expression.

4 Cut a thin strip of deep pink modelling paste and place this under the eyes to neaten the join and give the eyes a more 3D quality.

5 For the eyebrows, roll a 20cm (8in) long x 2cm (¾in) wide sausage from purple sugarpaste, using a smoother to give a uniform shape. Cut in half, then use the smoother to narrow one end of each to a width of 1.25cm (½in). Place on the cake so that the narrow end of one shaped sausage crosses the centre of the eyes and cut to fit. On the outer edge, mark how long you wish the brows to be, remove the paste and cut with a palette knife. Cut the second sausage to match and stick both in place. Add a little kitchen paper (paper towel) under the outer edge of each brow to support the paste while it dries.

6 To create the pale pink beading around the outside of the eye, knead pale pink modelling paste to warm and roll into a long sausage about 1cm (⅜in) thick. Place on top of the 8mm (⅝in) section of the perfect pearls mould and press into the mould

with firstly your fingers and then the back of a Dresden tool. Use a palette knife to cut away the excess paste and then release the beading by flexing the mould along its length so that the beads fall out without breaking or distorting. Allow to firm up a little before attaching with sugar glue.

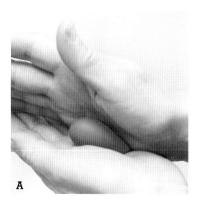

The beak and feet

1 For the beak, roll 20g (¾oz) of the orange modelling paste into a ball. Place the edge of the top hand next to the ball and roll the ball backwards and forwards until it turns into a cone (**Fig A**). Attach in place on the owl with sugar glue, referring to the finished cake for placement.

2 For the feet, roll six orange modelling paste cones using 10g (¼oz) of paste for each. Attach to the base of the owl with sugar glue (**Fig B**).

The finishing touch

Transfer the cake to the decorated board to complete.

You will need

owl cookies and cutter (LC)

30g (generous 1oz) sugarpaste (rolled fondant) per cookie, colours as for the main cake

modelling paste, colours as for the main cake

selection of embossers as for the main cake

cutters: heart from card suit set (LC); eight-petal flower from flat floral set 2 (LC); six-petal blossom from flat floral set 1 (LC), 3cm (1⅛in) circle

piping tubes (tips): nos. 18 and 4 (PME)

piping gel

Artful little owls

So many colours, so many possibilities – I would have loved to have made you a whole parliament of owls in lots of colour combinations to inspire you! However, I hope that my little owl character shows you what can be achieved with a few simple cutters and embossers. Although the owl in each picture is the same, which one you find most appealing is determined by the background colour on which it is displayed. I personally prefer the owl on the blue background, as the balance of the colours seems to work.

1 Roll out purple, lime green and very deep pink sugarpaste to a thickness of 5mm (⅛in), ideally using spacers. Cut out an owl shape from each colour using the cookie cutter.

2 Use a cutting wheel to cut out the eyes, the front and the wings from each of the sugarpastes.

3 Texture the wings using a couple of the embossers – I have used bee and blossom embossers.

4 Paint piping gel over each of the cookies as a glue and then reassemble the owls on the cookies using different-coloured sugarpastes for each section.

5 Emboss some thinly rolled-out modelling paste with flowers. Use the heart cutter to cut out one heart for each owl and attach in place.

6 Create the eyes using thinly rolled-out modelling paste and the suggested cutters.

7 Add eyebrows, beak and feet to each cookie, rolled from modelling paste as for the main cake.

tip TRY OUT DIFFERENT EMBOSSERS ON SOME SPARE SUGARPASTE TO SEE WHICH ONES YOU LIKE THE BEST.

COMPARE THE OWL ON THE BLUE BACKGROUND WITH THE ORANGE AND GREEN BACKGROUNDS, WHERE THE PURPLE WINGS APPEAR MUCH DARKER AND MUDDIER AND THE HEAD ALMOST DISAPPEARS INTO THE BACKGROUND. THE PINK BACKGROUND ON THE OTHER HAND GIVES THE OWL A LIGHTER, AIRIER FEEL, SO I GUESS SOME OF YOU WILL PREFER THIS ONE!

"Colour in certain places has the great value of making the outlines and structural planes seem more energetic" – Antonio Gaudi

113

... patchwork owl

FESTIVE
FIR

Colour inspiration...

Green is the colour of nature, growth and harmony, a restful colour that has become increasingly popular over the last few years. I must admit that green is not a colour I usually opt for when decorating my cakes, but for this Christmas tree cake I was inspired by the wonderful green necklace pictured below with its myriad greens, cool blue-greens, warm lime greens, dark recessive greens and light reflective greens. The gold disc detail adds a touch of glamour and reminded me of detailed vintage buttons. In colour theory terms, the necklace has an analogous colour scheme, as all the colours are adjacent to each other on the colour wheel.

THE FOREST GREENS, SPRING LIMES AND SPARKLING CRYSTALS OF THIS ATTRACTIVE NECKLACE CREATE A PERFECTLY BALANCED COLOUR SCHEME FOR A CAKE.

Necklace © Ladies Who Lunch Couture Jewellery
www.ladieswholunchjewellery.com

ANALOGOUS COLOUR SCHEME

WHITE AND GOLD STARS DECORATE A SHOP'S
ENTRANCE IN BARCELONA.

A DECORATIVE MIRROR OVER THE ENTRANCE
TO AN INTERIOR DESIGN SHOP, BARCELONA.

THE GREENS OF THIS GLASS LAMP ARE
WARMED BY THE LIGHT.

THE LIGHT REFLECTING OFF THIS SILVER
GREEN FOLIAGE TURNS IT ICY BLUE.

analogous colour scheme ...

1   2   3

4   5   6

7   8

Mixing the colours

To recreate the colours I have used, add the following paste colours to white sugarpaste or use the sugarpaste I have suggested:

1 gold: M&B ivory sugarpaste plus autumn leaf (SF)

2 dark green: M&B dark green sugarpaste plus bluebell (SK)

3 leaf green: M&B dark green sugarpaste and gooseberry (SF) plus a touch of bluebell (SK)

4 vibrant lime: vine (SK) and daffodil (SK) plus a touch of bluegrass (SK)

5 pale lime: vine (SK) and mint (SK) plus a touch of gooseberry (SF)

6 deep blue-green: bluegrass (SK)

7 pale blue-green: a touch of deep blue-green plus vibrant lime added to white sugarpaste

8 ivory: M&B ivory sugarpaste

You will need.

materials

cakes: 3 round cakes 10cm (4in), 15cm (6in) and 20cm (8in), all 7.5cm (3in) high

sugarpaste (rolled fondant): 800g (1lb 12oz) gold; 330g (11½oz) dark green; 1.2kg (2lb 10oz) leaf green

modelling paste: 75g (2¾oz) each gold, dark green, leaf green and vibrant lime; 50g (2oz) each deep blue-green, pale blue-green and ivory; 25g (1oz) pale lime

royal icing, for sticking

light gold metallic edible lustre dust (SK)

piping gel

sugar glue

equipment

cake boards: 1 round drum 28cm (11in); 2 round hardboards 7.5cm (3in) and 1 round hardboard 5cm (2in) for tree trunk spacers; 3 round hardboards 10cm (4in), 15cm (6in) and 20cm (8in) for cakes

polystyrene tree spacer set (LC) or 2 round polystyrene dummies 7.5cm (3in) and 1 round polystyrene dummy 5cm (2in)

15mm (⅝in) wide gold ribbon and non-toxic glue stick

6 dowels

Victorian Lace Top stencil (DS C361)

cutters: stylish stars (LC); Chinese scrolls set (LC)

moulds: patterned button mould set (AM); Christmas tree mould set (AM); garden mould set (AM); star mould (AM)

lace motifs embossing set 20 (HP)

... festive fir

Preparation

The cake board, trunk and moulded sugar decorations for this unique tree cake can all be completed well in advance.

Covering and decorating the board

1 Roll out the gold sugarpaste to a thickness of 5mm (⅕in), ideally using spacers, and use to cover your cake board. Trim the soft sugarpaste to size and immediately position the Victorian lace stencil centrally on top of the covered board.

2 Place a smoother on top of the stencil and press down firmly so that the sugarpaste is forced towards the upper surface of the stencil (**Fig A**). Repeat, repositioning the smoother each time so that the entire pattern of the stencil is embossed into the soft sugarpaste. Re-trim the board as required to give a neat finish.

3 Once the sugarpaste has dried, mix the light gold edible lustre dust with water to create a thick paint.

A

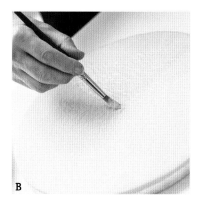

B

Then paint over the embossed board with radial strokes using a paintbrush (**Fig B**). Set aside to dry. Once dry, attach the gold ribbon to the board using a non-toxic glue stick.

Covering the trunk

1 If using cake dummies, take a sharp knife and reduce the heights to create one 7.5cm (3in) round and 5cm (2in) high, one 7.5cm (3in) round and 2.3cm (1in) high and one 5cm (2in) round and 1.8cm (¾in) high, double checking that each cut is level.

2 Using royal icing, stick each tree trunk spacer onto a round hardboard cake board of the same size and allow to set.

3 Place each spacer onto a square of waxed paper and cover with piping gel to help the sugarpaste stick to the surface.

4 Knead a small amount of the dark green sugarpaste until warm and pliable. Roll out to a depth of 5mm (⅕in), ideally using spacers, and use to cover one section of trunk.

5 You will find that the sugarpaste is thicker at the bottom of the section than the top, so to help overcome this, rotate the trunk between two flat-edged smoothers to redistribute the paste and ensure that the sides remain vertical (**Fig A**). Repeat for the remaining trunk sections.

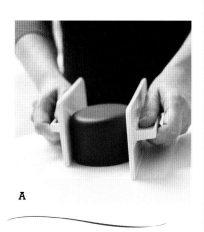

A

tip IF YOU PLAN TO USE EXCEPTIONALLY HEAVY CAKES, YOU CAN ALSO ADD DOWELS TO THE TRUNK AT THIS STAGE (SEE DOWELLING CAKES).

Making moulded shapes and cut-out stars

1 To make moulded buttons, knead a small amount of the gold modelling paste to warm it, then roll a ball of paste slightly larger than the button mould cavity you are using. Place the ball of paste into the mould, ensuring that the sugar surface being placed in the mould is perfectly smooth (**Fig A**); if there are small joins visible, they will probably be visible on your finished piece!

2 Push the paste into the mould firmly, then stroke the paste around the edges of the mould with your finger to help it fill the mould completely. Remove the excess paste with a palette knife so that the back of the mould is flat (**Fig B**).

3 To remove the paste, press a finger on the back of the mould under the button holes, then flex the mould back from the button to release (**Fig C**). Placing your finger under the button while flexing the mould ensures that the button holes are crisp and the mould doesn't drag and disfigure the sugar button.

4 Create a selection of moulded shapes as follows: trees using the deep blue-green modelling paste and the Christmas tree mould; small flowers using the pale lime and pale blue-green modelling pastes and the garden mould; and stars using the ivory modelling paste and the star mould (**Fig D**).

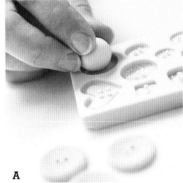

A

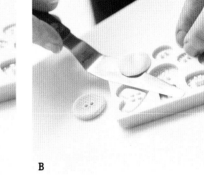

B

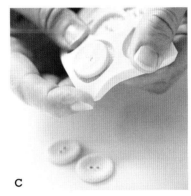

C

D

5 To create small stars, since the small ones in the mould are tricky to make, thinly roll out the ivory modelling paste between 1mm (¹⁄₃₂in) spacers and cut out shapes using the different sizes of stylish stars cutter. Place these and the moulded shapes on a foam pad to dry.

6 Once the buttons are dry, place them on a sheet of waxed paper and paint over them with the light gold lustre dust mixed with water to give them a shine and brilliance (**Fig E**).

E

... festive fir

Stage one

Carving and covering the cakes

1 Make circle templates from paper or card in the follow diameters: 15cm (6in), 10cm (4in), 7.5cm (3in) and 5cm (2in).

2 Take the remaining hardboard cake boards and, on the underside of each, draw a central circle using two of the templates, as follows: draw a 7.5cm (3in) diameter circle on the two larger sizes and a 5cm (2in) diameter circle on the smallest one (**Fig A**). These are to help when assembling the cake.

3 Turn all three hardboards over so that the circles are underneath and then place each cake on its respective hardboard.

4 Select one of the cakes and place the circle template that is 5cm (2in) smaller than the cake's diameter centrally on top of the cake. Using a knife, make a shallow cut around the board to mark its position so that if the board slips it is easier to replace. Next, carve from the edge of the template down to the edge of the board under the cake (**Fig B**). Do this in small cuts to ensure that you don't carve away too much cake. Repeat for the remaining two cakes.

5 To create the pointed top to the tree, take 70g (2½oz) of the remaining gold sugarpaste and mould it into a cone. Place the cone on top of the smallest tier and adjust the shape as necessary, using a smoother.

6 Place each cake on waxed paper and cover with leaf green sugarpaste (see Covering Cakes with Sugarpaste). For the upper tier, roll out the remaining sugarpaste into a strip and wrap around the cone. Cut away the excess where the paste joins with scissors and smooth the join closed. Remove the excess from the base as for the other tiers. Leave the paste to crust over, ideally overnight.

A

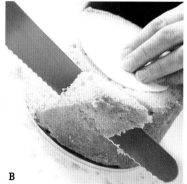

B

Stage two

Dowelling and stacking the cake

1 To dowel each cake, centre a paper template or board of the same size as the trunk spacer section above and, using a scriber, scribe around the edge of the template or board to leave a visible outline.

2 Dowel the cakes using three per cake (see Dowelling Cakes).

3 Assemble the cake using royal icing, referring to the drawn circles under each cake to aid placement. Note that you can move the cakes around quite freely while the royal icing is still wet, so you have a little time to make any necessary minor adjustments to the overall appearance of the cake.

4 Allow the royal icing to set firmly before decorating.

Stage three

Decorating the cake

1 Thinly roll out the vibrant lime modelling paste, ideally between 1mm (⅟₁₆in) spacers.

2 Take the multi leaf embosser from the lace motifs embossing set and, holding it between your thumb and index finger at right angles to the paste, press into the soft paste. Repeat, ensuring that you apply the same pressure each time so that the pattern has an even depth (**Fig A**).

3 Next, take the Chinese scrolls cutter set and cut out shapes using both sides of all three cutters to give you a selection of six different shapes (**Fig B**). Place the shapes under a stay fresh mat or plastic food bag to prevent them drying out.

4 Repeat using the leaf green modelling paste and the flower and scroll embosser and the dark green modelling paste and the single large leaf embosser to create a large selection of paste shapes in various sizes and colours.

5 Decorate the cake sides in sections, using sugar glue to attach the freshly cut and dried sugar shapes. Start at the top edge of a cake tier and position the shapes so that they slightly project above the top edge of the cake. Attach the Chinese scrolls, giving each shape a little movement (**Fig C**); do this by sticking sections only of a particular shape to the cake, allowing other sections to curve away from the cake surface.

A

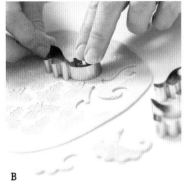

B

C

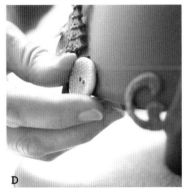

D

6 Attach a selection of scrolls and moulded shapes to the lower edge of the tier section you are working on, arranging them to disguise and soften the straight line of the edge (**Fig D**).

7 Fill in the area between the upper and lower edges, experimenting with the scrolls and placement of the moulded shapes as you go (**Fig E**).

8 Continue until the tree is completely covered.

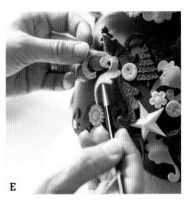

E

... festive fir

You will need

party cracker cookies and cutter (LC)

50g (2oz) sugarpaste (rolled fondant) per cookie, colours as for the main cake

modelling paste, colours as for the main cake

multi leaf embossers from lace motifs set 20 (HP)

patterned button mould set (AM)

light gold metallic edible lustre dust (SK)

4.5cm (1¾in) daisy/gerbera plunger cutter (PME)

piping gel

Christmas cookie crackers

These Christmas cracker-shaped cookies certainly add a festive touch and also illustrate the effect colour has on the overall appearance of the cookies. The pale icy colours used on the cracker at the back of this selection give a light, airy feel, but put the pale blue-green onto a dark green background and the cracker becomes very different and the pale flower now stands out vividly from its dark green background. Try experimenting with the various colourways to see which you prefer – you have lots to choose from – or simply make a mixed box as I have done so that there is one for everyone.

Covering and decorating the cookies

1 Cut out daisies from thinly rolled-out modelling paste in various colours, using the suggested cutter, and place on a foam pad to dry.

2 Make textured gold buttons as for the main cake, using the patterned button mould and the light gold edible lustre dust.

3 Roll out the sugarpaste to a thickness of 5mm (⅓in), ideally using spacers, and cut out cracker shapes using the cookie cutter used to create the cookies.

4 Emboss the ends of each cracker with the multi leaf embosser.

5 Paint piping gel over the top of the baked cookies to act as glue.

6 Carefully lift the sugarpaste shapes with a palette knife and place on top of the cookies.

7 Take a Dresden tool and, using the more pointed end, emboss short lines into the sugarpaste of each cracker to represent the gathered sections, as seen in the photo.

8 Decorate each cookie with a daisy of a different colour and top with a gold button.

tip IF THE COOKIE CUTTER HAS LEFT A RAGGED EDGE AROUND THE BASE OF A SHAPE, JUST CAREFULLY TUCK THIS UNDER WITH A FINGER BEFORE PLACING ON THE CAKE.

"The purest and most thoughtful minds are those which love colour the most" – John Ruskin

THESE CHRISTMAS COOKIE CRACKERS ILLUSTRATE HOW COMBINING THE SAME COLOURS IN DIFFERENT PROPORTIONS CAN COMPLETELY CHANGE THE MOOD AND APPEARANCE - ON THE ONE HAND CREATING A LIGHT, ICY, ETHEREAL CRACKER AND ON THE OTHER A BOLD, DOMINANT ONE.

... festive fir

basics

Equipment

You will find the following list of equipment useful when baking and decorating cakes and cookies. Specialist sugarcraft equipment such as embossers, stencil moulds and so on can be seen in action in the step photography throughout the book.

Bowls in various sizes for mixing

Cake boards:

◊ Drum – a thick board to display cakes (**1**)

◊ Hardboard – a thin strong board used in the construction of stacked cakes (**2**)

Cake stand for displaying completed cakes (**3**)

Carving knives – sharp, long-bladed pastry knives for levelling cakes and carving shapes

Small sharp knife for cutting paste

Cocktail sticks (toothpicks) used as markers and to transfer small amounts of paste colour (**4**)

Cookie cutters – available in a wide variety of shapes for cutting out cookies (**5**)

Foam pad (PME) used as a surface for thinning petals (not pictured)

Measuring spoons for accurate measurement of ingredients

Paintbrushes – in a range of sizes, for stippling, painting and dusting

Piping tubes (tips) for piping using a reusable piping (pastry) bag and coupler, using in a sugar shaper and to cut small circles (**6**)

Rolling pins, both large and small, for rolling out the different types of paste (**7**)

Scissors for cutting templates and trimming paste to shape

Set square for accurate alignment (**8**)

Spacers – 5mm (⅕in) and 1mm (¹⁄₃₂in) for rolling out paste (**9**)

Stay fresh mat for preventing rolled-out paste from drying out (**10**)

Tins (pans) for baking cakes: ball, round, multi-sized square and cupcake pan; UK cakes are traditionally 7.5cm (3in) high

Tools:

◊ Ball tool (FMM) to soften the edges of petals (**11**)
◊ Craft knife for intricate cutting tasks (**12**)
◊ Cutting wheel (PME) to use instead of a knife to avoid dragging the paste (**13**)
◊ Dresden tool to create markings on paste (**14**)
◊ Cranked-handled palette knives for spreading icing and cutting and lifting paste (**15**)
◊ Scriber (PME) for scribing around templates, popping air bubbles in paste and removing small sections of paste (**16**)
◊ Smoother to help create a smooth and even finish to sugarpaste (**17**)
◊ Sugar shaper and discs to create pieces of uniformly shaped modelling paste (**18**)

Work board – large and small non-stick, used for rolling out pastes

Wooden spoon to help mix buttercream, ganache, etc.

Wire rack for cooling cookies and cupcakes after baking

Measurements the world over

For readers who prefer to use US cup measurements, please use the following conversions (note: 1 tbsp = 15ml but 1 Australian tbsp = 20ml):

Butter 115g (4oz) = 1 stick/½ cup, 225g (8oz) = 2 sticks/1 cup, 25g (1oz) = 2 tbsp, 15g (½oz) = 1 tbsp

Caster (superfine) sugar 200g (7oz) = 1 cup, 25g (1oz) = 2 tbsp

Plain (all-purpose)/self-raising (-rising) flour 125g (4½oz) = 1 cup

Icing (confectioners') sugar 115g (4oz) = 1 cup

Liquid 250ml/9fl oz = 1 cup, 125ml (4fl oz) = ½ cup

Soft brown sugar 210g (7½oz) = 1 cup

Piping tubes
The following piping tubes (tips) have been used in the book. As tube numbers may vary with different suppliers, always check the tube diameter:

Tube no. (PME)	Diameter
0	0.5mm (0.020in)
1	1mm (¹⁄₃₂in)
1.5	1.2mm (¹⁄₃₂in)
2	1.5mm (¹⁄₁₆in)
3	2mm (³⁄₃₂in)
4	2mm (³⁄₃₂in)
16	5mm (³⁄₁₆in)
17	6mm (¼in)
18	7mm (⁵⁄₃₂in)

Lining tins

There are cake-release sprays on the market that you can use, but I still prefer the traditional method of lining tins (pans). Neatly lined tins will prevent the cake mixture from sticking and help ensure a good shape. Use a good-quality baking parchment (parchment paper) that is designed for the purpose. The paper should always sit right up against the sides of the tin with no large air pockets. Also, watch the uppermost side edge of the paper, as you don't want this protruding into the cake itself, so secure it with a little fat or a small fold in the paper.

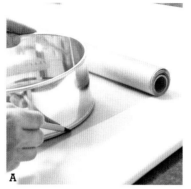

A   **B**

Straight-sided round and square tins

1 Place your tin on the top of some baking parchment, draw around the base with a pencil (**Fig A**) and cut out the resulting shape with scissors.

2 Measure the circumference of your tin and cut a strip of baking parchment slightly longer than this measurement to allow for an overlap. Make the strip 5cm (2in) deeper than the height of the tin. Fold up 2.5cm (1in) along the bottom of the strip. Make diagonal cuts into the folded-over section of the paper that goes around the sides to enable the paper to sit snugly around the sides of the tin (**Fig B**).

C

3 Grease the tin and place the strip around the sides, with the cut edge at the bottom. Then place the parchment for the base on top (**Fig C**).

Baking cakes

The cake under the icing is vitally important – it needs to be moist, able to support the added weight of the icing and above all taste fantastic. Here are two of my tried and tested recipes for you to experiment with – enjoy.

Delicious chocolate fudge cake

As the name suggests, this is a delicious, moist chocolate cake, ideal for both carving and covering with sugarpaste. The secret with this recipe is to use good-quality chocolate with a high percentage of cocoa solids – don't be tempted to use cheap, low cocoa solids chocolate or even supermarket baking chocolate because you simply won't achieve the rich depth of flavour that this cake demands. This cake will keep for up to 10 days. For tips and comments about baking this cake, please visit the Lindy's Cakes blog.

Round	10cm (4in)	12.5cm (5in)	15cm (6in)	18cm (7in)	20cm (8in)	23cm (9in)	25.5cm (10in)	28cm (11in)
Square	7.5cm (3in)	10cm (4in)	12.5cm (5in)	15cm (6in)	18cm (7in)	20cm (8in)	23cm (9in)	25.5cm (10in)
Unsalted butter	75g (2¾oz)	110g (3¾oz)	140g (5oz)	180g (6oz)	225g (8oz)	280g (10oz)	340g (11¾oz)	450g (1lb)
Good-quality chocolate	75g (2¾oz)	110g (3¾oz)	140g (5oz)	180g (6oz)	225g (8oz)	280g (10oz)	340g (11¾oz)	450g (1lb)
Instant coffee granules	1 tsp	1½ tsp	2 tsp	2¼ tsp	1 tbsp	1¼ tbsp	1½ tbsp	2 tbsp
Caster (superfine) sugar or soft brown sugar	150g (5½oz)	225g (8oz)	280g (10oz)	360g (12½oz)	450g (1lb)	560g (1lb 4oz)	675g (1lb 8oz)	900g (2lb)
Water	50ml (2fl oz)	75ml (2½fl oz)	95ml (3¼fl oz)	120ml (4fl oz)	150ml (5fl oz)	190ml (6½fl oz)	225ml (8fl oz)	300ml (10fl oz)
Large eggs (US extra large)	1.3	2	2½	3	4	5	6	8
Vegetable oil	2 tsp (10ml)	4 tsp (20ml)	4 tsp (20ml)	2 tbsp (30ml)	35ml (1.1fl oz)	45ml (1¾fl oz)	50ml (2fl oz)	70ml (2½fl oz)
Sour cream (or natural/plain yogurt or crème fraîche)	40ml (1½fl oz)	50ml (2fl oz)	60ml (2¼fl oz)	80ml (2½fl oz)	100ml (3½fl oz)	125ml (4fl oz)	150ml (5fl oz)	200ml (7fl oz)
Self-raising (-rising) flour	40g (1½oz)	60g (2¼oz)	80g (3oz)	100g (3½oz)	125g (4½oz)	160g (5¾oz)	190g (6¾oz)	250g (9oz)
Plain (all-purpose) flour	40g (1½oz)	60g (2¼oz)	80g (3oz)	100g (3½oz)	125g (4½oz)	160g (5¾oz)	190g (6¾oz)	250g (9oz)
Cocoa powder (unsweetened cocoa)	15g (½oz)	25g (1oz)	30g (generous 1oz)	40g (1½oz)	50g (2oz)	65g (2¼oz)	75g (2¾oz)	100g (3½oz)
Bicarbonate of soda (baking soda)	¼ tsp	¼ tsp .	¼ tsp	⅜ tsp	½ tsp	½ tsp	¾ tsp	1 tsp
Baking times	1 hour 5 mins	1 hour 10 mins	1¼ hours	1½ hours	1¾ hours	2 hours	2 hours 10 mins	2 hours 20 mins

1 Preheat your oven to 160°C/325°F/ Gas Mark 3. Grease and line the cake tin (pan).

2 Slowly melt the butter and chocolate with the coffee, sugar and water in a saucepan, then allow to cool.

3 Add the eggs, oil and sour cream to the mixture and stir well.

4 Sift all the dry ingredients into a large bowl and make a well in the centre of the ingredients.

5 Pour the chocolate mixture into well and mix until the ingredients are thoroughly combined.

6 Pour the batter into the lined tin and bake for the required time or until a skewer inserted into the centre of the cake comes out clean. Remember that all ovens are different, so do check your cake towards the end of its baking time.

7 Leave the cake to cool completely in the tin.

... basics

Madeira cake

A firm, moist cake that can be flavoured to suit a variety of tastes or occasions. It is ideal for both carving and covering with sugarpaste, and will keep for up to two weeks. For in-depth tips and discussion on how to bake the perfect Madeira cake, please visit the Lindy's Cakes blog.

Cake sizes		Unsalted butter	Caster (superfine) sugar	Self-raising (-rising) flour	Plain (all-purpose) flour	Large eggs (US extra large)	Baking times
10cm (4in) round/ball	7.5cm (3in) square	75g (2¾oz)	75g (2¾oz)	75g (2¾oz)	40g (1½oz)	1½	45 mins–1 hour
12.5cm (5in) round	10cm (4in) square	115g (4oz)	115g (4oz)	115g (4oz)	50g (2oz)	2	45 mins–1 hour
15cm (6in) round	12.5cm (5in) square/ball	175g (6oz)	175g (6oz)	175g (6oz)	175g (6oz)	3	1–1¼ hours
18cm (7in) round	15cm (6in) square	225g (8oz)	225g (8oz)	225g (8oz)	125g (4½oz)	4	1–1¼ hours
20cm (8in) round	18cm (7in) square/15cm (6in) ball	350g (12oz)	350g (12oz)	350g (12oz)	175g (6oz)	6	1¼–1½ hours
23cm (9in) round	20cm (8in) square	450g (1lb)	450g (1lb)	450g (1lb)	225g (8oz)	8	1½–1¾ hours
25.5cm (10in) round	23cm (9in) square	500g (1lb 2oz)	500g (1lb 2oz)	500g (1lb 2oz)	250g (9oz)	9	1½–1¾ hours
28cm (11in)	25.5cm (10in) square	700g (1lb 9oz)	700g (1lb 9oz)	700g (1lb 9oz)	350g (12oz)	12	1¾–2 hours
30cm (12in) round	28cm (11in) square	850g (1lb 14oz)	850g (1lb 14oz)	850g (1lb 14oz)	425g (15oz)	15	2–2¼ hours
33cm (13in) round	30cm (12in) square	1kg (2lb 4oz)	1kg (2lb 4oz)	1kg (2lb 4oz)	500g (1lb 2oz)	18	2¼–2½ hours
35.5cm (14in) round	33cm (13in) square	1.2kg (2lb 10oz)	1.2kg (2lb 10oz)	1.2kg (2lb 10oz)	600g (1lb 5oz)	21	2½–2¾ hours

tip CAREFULLY BREAK EACH EGG INTO A CUP TO PREVENT SMALL PIECES OF EGGSHELL FALLING INTO THE BATTER.

1 Preheat the oven to 160°C/325°F/ Gas Mark 3. Grease and line the cake tin (pan). To prevent the sides of the cake crusting and the top doming, tie a double layer of brown paper or newspaper around the outside of the tin, or use one of the commercial products available for this purpose.

2 Beat the butter and sugar together until light, fluffy and very pale – I find this takes about 5 minutes in an electric mixer. Sift the flours together into a separate bowl.

3 Beat the eggs, which should be at room temperature, into the creamed mixture, one at a time, following each with a spoonful of the flour to prevent the mixture curdling.

4 Sift the remaining flour into the creamed mixture and fold in carefully with a large metal spoon. Add the flavouring, if using. At this stage you can add glycerine to help keep the cake moist – you will need ¼ teaspoon per egg.

5 Transfer to the lined tin and bake for the required time or until well risen, firm to the touch and a skewer inserted into the centre comes out clean. You may need to protect the top of your cake during baking to prevent it crusting too much – I usually put a baking sheet on the shelf above my cake throughout the baking process.

6 Leave the cake to cool completely in the tin. Then, leaving the lining paper on, wrap the cake in foil or place in an airtight container for at least 12 hours before cutting, to allow the cake to settle.

Flavourings
Traditionally, Madeira cake was flavoured with lemon, but it can also be made with other flavourings, as follows. The amounts given are for a six-egg quantity of cake mixture; increase or decrease the amounts for other quantities.

Lemon grated zest of 2 lemons
Vanilla 5ml (1 tsp) vanilla extract
Cherry 350g (12oz) glacé (candied) cherries, halved
Fruit 350g (12oz) sultanas (golden raisins), currants, raisins or chopped stoned dates
Coconut 110g (3¾oz) desiccated (dry unsweetened shredded) coconut
Almond 5ml (1 tsp) almond extract and 3 tbsp ground almonds

tip IF YOU HAVE A FAVOURITE RECIPE THAT YOU WOULD LIKE TO USE BUT IT'S NOT FOR THE SIZE OF CAKE YOU NEED, PLEASE VISIT THE LINDY'S CAKES BLOG AND CLICK ON THE FAQS SECTION WHERE YOU WILL FIND A CHART TO HELP YOU ADAPT YOUR RECIPE.

Using a ball tin

Sponge cake balls are baked in two halves in separate half-sphere tins, and special care must be taken when lining these tins.

Ball tins

1 Cut two circles of the appropriate size from baking parchment: 15cm (6in) for a 10cm (4in) ball; 20cm (8in) for a 12.5cm (5in) ball; and 25.5cm (10in) for a 15cm (6in) ball.

2 Fold the circles into quarters and then fold again so that the circles are folded and marked into eighths. Open out until folded into quarters once more and then cut along the fold lines into the centre.

3 Grease both the tin and one side of the fully opened-out paper and place each circle into the centre of one half of the tin, greased sides together. Encourage the paper to fit the tin by overlapping the sections.

4 Divide the cake batter between two lined ball tins for baking. Once baked, allow the halves to cool in the tin, then level each cake using the edge of the tin (see Levelling Cakes) and stick the two halves together to create a perfect sphere.

Baking cupcakes

Baking cupcakes should be fun! First of all, choose your cupcake cases (liners) and then select a recipe to use. All the cake recipes in this book work as cupcakes, but you can use any cake recipe, so please don't be afraid to experiment. Below is one of my current favourite cupcake recipes, but if you would like a few more, take a look at my *Bake me I'm yours… Cupcake Celebration* book or the recipe section on the Lindy's Cakes blog.

Mojito cupcakes

These delicate cupcakes have a wonderful flavour and a flat top that is perfect for decorating with sugarpaste. They are best eaten within 3 days.

Makes 20-24 cupcakes

6 sprigs of fresh mint

150ml (5fl oz) hot milk

125g (4½oz) butter, softened

200g (7oz) caster (superfine) sugar

2 large eggs (US extra large), at room temperature

grated zest of 2 limes

2.5ml (½ tsp) vanilla extract

30ml (2 tbsp) light or dark rum

210g (7½oz) self-raising (-rising) flour, sifted

1 Preheat the oven to 170°C/325°F/ Gas Mark 3 and line two bun or muffin trays (pans) with paper cupcake cases (liners).

2 Add the mint leaves to the hot milk and leave them to steep. How long you steep the mint will depend on how minty you wish your cupcakes to be – I often leave mine until the milk has cooled, but 15 minutes or so should be long enough for a delicate flavour to develop.

3 Beat the butter and sugar together until light, fluffy and very pale – I find this takes about 5 minutes in an electric mixer.

4 Beat the eggs into the creamed mixture, one at a time, following each with a spoonful of the flour to prevent the mixture curdling.

5 Add the lime zest, vanilla and rum to the cooled milk.

6 Using a large metal spoon, fold the flour and milk mixture alternately into the creamed mixture, ending with the flour.

7 Spoon the cake mixture into the cupcake cases until about half full.

8 Bake for about 20 minutes or until a fine skewer inserted into the centres comes out clean.

9 Leave the cupcakes to cool for 5 minutes before removing them to a wire rack to cool completely.

Baking cookies

Fundamental to any decorated cookie is the taste and shape of the cookie itself. When choosing a recipe, it is important to opt for one that retains its shape and doesn't spread too much while baking. Other exciting cookie recipes can be found in my *Bake me I'm yours… Cookie* book.

Vanilla cookies

Bake perfect cookies every time with this easy recipe. Try replacing the golden syrup with honey for a different flavour, or adding grated orange or lemon zest for a citrus tang.

Makes about 20 cookies

275g (9oz) plain (all-purpose) flour, sifted, plus extra for dusting

1 tsp baking powder

100g (3½oz) caster (superfine) sugar

75g (2¾oz) butter, diced

1 small egg, beaten

30ml (2 tbsp) golden syrup (or dark corn syrup)

2.5ml (½ tsp) vanilla extract

1 Preheat the oven to 170°C/325°F/Gas Mark 3.

2 Place the dry ingredients in a large bowl.

3 Add the butter and rub into the dry ingredients with your fingertips until the mixture resembles fine breadcrumbs.

4 Make a hollow in the centre and pour in the beaten egg, syrup and vanilla extract. Mix together well until you have a ball of dough.

5 Place the cookie dough in a plastic bag and then chill in the fridge for 30 minutes.

6 Roll the dough out on a lightly floured surface to 5mm (⅕in) thick and use your chosen cutters to stamp out the cookies.

7 Lightly knead the trimmings together and re-roll to use up all the dough.

8 Place the cookies on baking (cookie) sheets.

9 Bake the cookies for 12–15 minutes until lightly coloured and firm but not crisp.

10 Leave the cookies to cool for 5 minutes before removing them to a wire rack to cool completely.

Sugar recipes

Most of the sugar recipes used in the book for covering, modelling and decoration can easily be made at home.

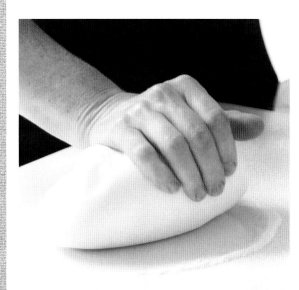

Sugarpaste

Used to cover cakes and boards, ready-made sugarpaste (rolled fondant) can be obtained from supermarkets and cake decorating suppliers, and is available in white and the whole colour spectrum. It is also easy and inexpensive to make your own.

Makes 1kg (2lb 4oz)

60ml (4 tbsp) cold water

20ml (4 tsp/1 sachet) powdered gelatine

125ml (4fl oz) liquid glucose (glucose syrup)

15ml (1 tbsp) glycerine

1kg (2lb 4oz) icing (confectioners') sugar, sifted, plus extra for dusting

1 Place the cold water in a small heatproof bowl, sprinkle over the gelatine and leave to soak until spongy. Stand the bowl over a saucepan of hot but not boiling water and stir until the gelatine is dissolved. Add the glucose and glycerine, stirring until well blended and runny.

2 Place the icing sugar in a large bowl. Make a well in the centre and slowly pour in the liquid ingredients, stirring constantly. Mix well. Turn out onto a surface dusted with icing sugar and knead until smooth, sprinkling with extra icing sugar if the paste becomes too sticky. The paste can be used immediately or tightly wrapped and stored in a plastic bag until required.

tip FOR COMMENTS AND TIPS ON MAKING YOUR OWN SUGARPASTE, PLEASE VISIT THE LINDY'S CAKE BLOG.

Modelling paste

Used to add decoration to cakes, this versatile paste keeps its shape well, drying harder than sugarpaste (rolled fondant). Although there are commercial modelling pastes available, it is easy and a lot less expensive to make your own by simply adding gum tragacanth, a natural gum available from cake decorating suppliers, to sugarpaste.

Makes 50g (2oz)

50g (2oz) sugarpaste (rolled fondant)

¼ tsp gum tragacanth

1 Make a well in the sugarpaste and add the gum tragacanth, then knead in.

2 Wrap in a plastic bag and allow the gum to work before use. You will begin to feel a difference in the paste after an hour or so, but it is best left overnight. The modelling paste should be firm but pliable with a slight elastic texture. Kneading the modelling paste makes it warm and easy to work with.

tips...

IF TIME IS SHORT, USE CMC INSTEAD OF GUM TRAGACANTH; THIS IS A SYNTHETIC PRODUCT BUT IT WORKS ALMOST STRAIGHT AWAY.

PLACING YOUR MODELLING PASTE IN A MICROWAVE FOR A FEW SECONDS IS AN EXCELLENT WAY OF WARMING IT FOR USE.

IF YOU HAVE PREVIOUSLY ADDED A LARGE AMOUNT OF COLOUR TO YOUR PASTE AND IT IS THEN TOO SOFT, AN EXTRA PINCH OR TWO OF GUM TRAGACANTH WILL BE NECESSARY.

IF YOUR PASTE IS CRUMBLY OR TOO HARD TO WORK, ADD A TOUCH OF WHITE VEGETABLE FAT (SHORTENING) AND A LITTLE COOLED BOILED WATER, AND KNEAD UNTIL SOFTENED.

White vegetable fat

This is a solid white vegetable fat (shortening) that is often known by a brand name: in the UK, Trex or White Flora; in South Africa, Holsum; in Australia, Copha; and in America, Crisco. These products are more or less interchangeable in cake making.

Buttercream

Buttercream has many uses: as a filling between layers of cake, as a glue to attach sugarpaste (rolled fondant) to cakes and as a topping on cupcakes. There are quite a few different recipes for buttercream, but here is a standard one, with suggestions for a variety of flavourings.

Makes 450g (1lb)

110g (3¾oz) unsalted butter, softened

350g (12oz) icing (confectioners') sugar

15–30ml (1–2 tbsp) milk or water

a few drops of vanilla extract or alternative flavouring

1 Place the butter in a bowl and beat until light and fluffy.

2 Sift the icing sugar into the bowl and continue to beat until the mixture changes colour.

3 Add just enough milk or water to the mixture to give a firm but spreadable consistency.

4 Flavour by adding the vanilla or alternative flavouring, then store the buttercream in an airtight container until required.

Flavourings
Try replacing the liquid in the recipes with:

Spirits such as whisky, rum or brandy
Other liquid flavourings such as coffee, melted chocolate, lemon curd or fresh fruit purées
Nut butters to make a praline flavour
Aromatic flavourings such as mint or rose extract

Chocolate ganache

Used as a filling or coating for cakes, I also like to use ganache on cupcakes. A must for all chocoholics – use the best chocolate you can source for a really indulgent topping.

Makes 400g (14oz)

Dark chocolate ganache

200g (7oz) good-quality dark (bittersweet) chocolate

200ml (7fl oz) double (heavy) cream

Makes 280g (9½oz)

White chocolate ganache

200g (7oz) good-quality white chocolate

80ml (2½fl oz) double (heavy) cream

1 Melt the chocolate and cream in a heatproof bowl over a saucepan of gently simmering water, stirring to combine. Alternatively, melt in a microwave on low power, stirring thoroughly every 20 seconds or so.

2 Leave the ganache until it has thickened slightly and is of a pouring consistency, or leave to cool so that it can be spread with a palette knife. Alternatively, once cooled completely it can be whisked to give a lighter texture.

Quick royal icing

Use royal icing for stencil work, constructing stacked cakes and piping fine details.

Makes 250g (9oz)

1 large egg white (US extra large)

250g (9oz) icing (confectioners') sugar, sifted

1 Place the egg white in a bowl and lightly beat until it has broken down, then gradually beat in the icing sugar until the icing is glossy and forms soft peaks.

2 Store your royal icing in an airtight container – cover the top surface with clingfilm (plastic wrap) and then a clean damp cloth to prevent the icing forming a crust, before adding the lid and placing in the fridge.

3 Before using the icing, bring it to room temperature and paddle the icing on your work board with a palette knife to remove any trapped air bubbles.

Glues

You can often just use water to stick your sugar decorations to your cakes, but if you find you need something a little stronger, here are two alternative options:

Sugar glue

This is a quick, easy and instant glue to make and is my preferred choice.

Break up pieces of white modelling paste into a small container and cover with boiling water. Stir until dissolved. This produces a thick, strong glue that can be easily thinned by adding some more cooled boiled water. If a stronger glue is required, use pastillage rather than modelling paste as the base – useful for delicate work.

Gum glue

Clear gum glue is available commercially, often known as edible glue or sugarcraft glue, but it is very easy and much less expensive to make it yourself.

The basic ingredients for the glue are 1 part CMC to 20 parts warm water, which translates into ¼ teaspoon gum to 2 tablespoons (30ml) warm water. Place the CMC in a small container with a lid, add the warm water and shake well. Leave the mixture in the fridge overnight. In the morning you will have a thick, clear glue that can be used to stick your sugar work together.

Preparing cakes and boards

Follow these basic techniques to achieve a neat and professional appearance to the initial cake and board coverings. With care and practice you will soon find that you have a perfectly smooth finish.

Levelling cakes

Making an accurate cake base is an important part of creating your masterpiece. There are two ways to do this, depending on the cake:

Method 1

Place a set square up against the edge of the cake and, with a sharp knife, mark a line around the top of the cake at the required height: 7–7.5cm (2¾–3in). With a large serrated knife, cut around the marked line and across the cake to remove the domed crust.

Method 2

Place a cake board in the base of the tin (pan) in which the cake was baked so that when the cake is placed on top, the outer edge of the cake will be level with the tin and the dome will protrude above. Take a long, sharp knife and cut the dome from the cake, keeping the knife against the tin. This will ensure that the cake is completely level. **Note:** This method is only suitable if the tin in which you baked your cake is 7.5cm (3in) high.

Filling cakes

It is not necessary to add fillings to the cake recipes used in this book, but many people do like their sponge cakes filled with jam and/or buttercream. To add filling(s), split the cake into a number of horizontal layers and spread each layer with your choice of filling.

Curving the top edge of cakes

If your cake is particularly crusty or you wish to neaten the top edge of the cake to give it a smooth curved appearance, take a pair of scissors and carefully cut small sections of cake away from the top edge. You can use a knife to do this, but scissors ensure that only small uniform amounts of cake are removed.

Covering cakes with sugarpaste

1 Using a palette knife, cover the cake with a thin layer of soft buttercream to fill in any holes and help the sugarpaste (rolled fondant) stick to the surface (**Fig A**).

2 Knead the sugarpaste until warm and pliable. Roll out on a surface lightly smeared with white vegetable fat (shortening), rather than icing (confectioners') sugar (fat works well and you don't have the problems of the sugar drying out or marking the sugarpaste), to a depth of 5mm (⅕in). It is a good idea to use spacers for this, as they will ensure an even thickness (**Fig B**).

3 Lift the paste carefully over the top of the cake, supporting it with a rolling pin, and position it so that it covers the cake (**Fig C**). Use a smoother to smooth the top surface of the cake to remove any lumps and bumps. Then smooth the top edge with the palm of your hand – always make sure your hands are clean and dry with no traces of cake crumbs before smoothing sugarpaste.

4 Using a cupped hand and an upward movement, encourage the sugarpaste on the sides of the cake to adjust to the shape of your cake (**Fig D**).

5 Don't press down on any pleats in the paste; instead, open them out and redistribute the paste until the cake is completely covered. Smooth the sides using a smoother.

6 Take the smoother and, while pressing down, run the flat edge around the base of the cake to create a cutting line (**Fig E**). Trim away the excess paste with a palette knife to create a neat edge (**Fig F**).

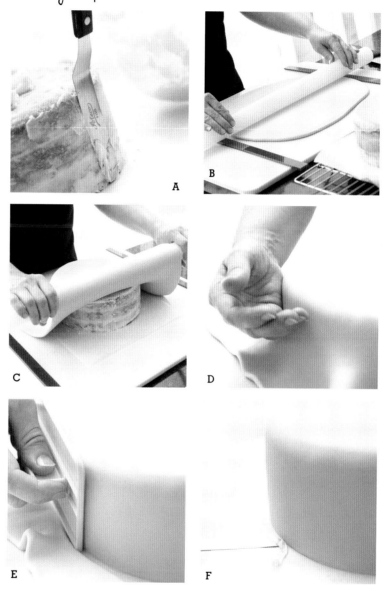

A

B

C

D

E

F

tip IF YOU FIND THAT YOU HAVE UNWANTED BUBBLES UNDER THE ICING, INSERT A SCRIBER AT AN ANGLE AND PRESS OUT THE AIR.

Covering boards with sugarpaste

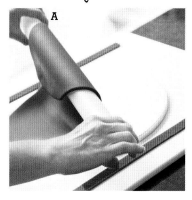

A

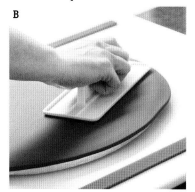

B

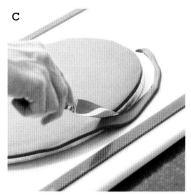

C

1 Roll out the sugarpaste (rolled fondant) to a depth of 5mm (⅛in), ideally using spacers.

2 Moisten the edge of the board with water or sugar glue. Lift up the paste and drape over the board (**Fig A**).

3 Circle a smoother over the paste to achieve a smooth, flat finish to the board (**Fig B**).

4 Using a cranked-handled palette knife, cut the paste flush with the sides of the board, taking care to keep the edge vertical (**Fig C**). The covered board should ideally be left overnight to dry thoroughly.

tip HOLD THE PALETTE KNIFE AT 45 DEGREES IN ORDER TO ACHIEVE A CLEAN CUT.

Cake construction

A multi-tiered cake, like a building, needs a structure hidden within it to prevent it from collapsing. It is important that this structure is 'built' correctly to take the loads put upon it, so please follow the instructions in the projects carefully, as it is worth the time involved to get this stage correct.

Dowelling cakes

All but the top cake will usually need dowelling to provide support. It is essential that all the dowels are inserted vertically, all are the same length and all have flat tops, and also that all the cakes being stacked have hardboards beneath them.

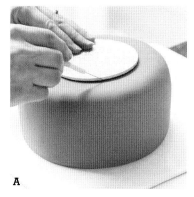

A

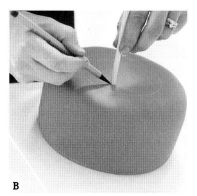

B

1 To dowel a cake, centre a cake board the same size as the tier above and scribe around the edge of the board to leave a visible outline (**Fig A**).

2 Insert a dowel 2.5cm (1in) in from the scribed line vertically down through the cake to the cake board below. Make a pencil mark or knife scratch on the dowel to mark the exact height (**Fig B**), then remove the dowel.

3 Take a sharp cutter – I am using a ratcheted pipe cutter here – and cut cleanly across the dowel, using the pencil mark to guide you (**Fig C**).

4 Cut two or more dowels to the same length.

5 Place the first dowel back in the measuring hole and insert the other dowels, evenly spaced, within the scribed circle (**Fig D**).

6 Repeat for all but the top cake.

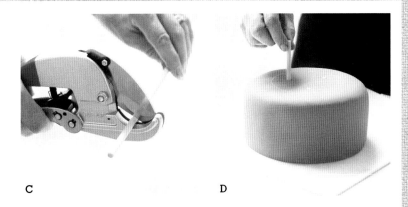

C   D

Stacking cakes

Cover and dowel each cake before stacking. Place 1 tablespoon (15ml) royal icing within the scribed area of the base cake and stack the next-sized cake on top, using the scribed line as a placement guide. Repeat the same process with the remaining cakes.

Storing decorated cakes and cookies
The following conditions will affect your decorated cakes and cookies:

Sunlight will fade and alter the colours of icing, so always ensure you store in a dark place.

Humidity can have a disastrous effect on modelling paste decorations, causing the icing to become soft and to droop if freestanding. It can also cause dark colours to bleed into lighter colours.

Heat can melt icing, especially buttercream, and prevent sugarpaste (rolled fondant) crusting over.

... basics

Abbreviations used in this book

AM – Alphabet Moulds
DS – Designer Stencils
FI – First Impressions
FMM – FMM Sugarcraft
GI – Great Impressions

HP – Holly Products
JEM – JEM Cutters cc
LC – Lindy's Cakes Ltd
OP – Orchard Products
PC – Patchwork Cutters

PME – PME Sugarcraft
SF – Sugarflair
SK – Squires Kitchen

Suppliers

UK

Lindy's Cakes Ltd (LC)
Unit 2, Station Approach,Wendover,
Bucks HP22 6BN
Tel: +44(0)1296 622418
www.lindyscakes.co.uk
Manufacturer of cutters and stencils plus online shop
for equipment used in this and Lindy's other books

Alan Silverwood Limited
Ledsam House, Ledsam Street,
Birmingham B16 8DN
Tel: +44(0)121 454 3571
www.alansilverwood.co.uk
Manufacturer of multi mini cake pans
and spherical moulds/ball tins (pans)

FMM Sugarcraft (FMM)
Unit 7, Chancerygate Business Park,
Whiteleaf Road, Hemel Hempstead,
Herts HP3 9HD
Tel: +44(0)1442 292970
www.fmmsugarcraft.com
Manufacturer of cutters

Holly Products (HP)
Primrose Cottage, Church Walk,
Norton in Hales,
Shropshire TF9 4QX
Tel/Fax: +44(0)1630 655759
www.hollyproducts.co.uk
Manufacturer and supplier of
embossing sticks and moulds

M&B of London
3a Millmead Industrial Estate,
Mill Mead Road,
London N17 9QU
Tel: +44(0)20 8801 7948
www.mbsc.co.uk
Manufacturer and supplier of
sugarpaste

Patchwork Cutters (PC)
Unit 12, Arrowe Commercial Park,
Arrowe Brook Road, Upton, Wirral
CH49 1AB
Tel/Fax: +44(0)151 678 5053
www.patchworkcutters.co.uk
Manufacturer and supplier of cutters
and embossers

Squires Kitchen
3 Waverley Lane, Farnham,
Surrey GU9 8BB
Tel: 0845 61 71 810
www.squires-shop.com/uk
Manufacturer and supplier of paste
colours and other edibles

Stitch Craft Create
Brunel House, Newton Abbot,
Devon TQ12 4PU
Tel: +44(0)844 880 5852
www.stitchcraftcreate.co.uk
Supplier of cake baking and
decorating equipment and books

US

Global Sugar Art
1509 Military Turnpike,
Plattsburgh, NY 12901
Tel: 1-518-561-3039 or
1-800-420-6088
www.globalsugarart.com
Sugarcraft supplier that imports many
UK products into the US

Cake Craft Shoppe
3554 Highway 6
Sugar Land, Texas 77478
Tel: 281-491-3920
www.cakecraftshoppe.com
Sugarcraft supplier that imports many
UK products into the US

First Impressions Molds
300 Business Park Way, Suite A-200,
Royal Palm Beach, FL 33411
Tel: 561-784-7186
www.firstimpressionsmolds.com
Manufacturer and supplier of
handcrafted silicone moulds

Australia

Iced affair
53 Church Street,
Camperdown, NSW 2050
Tel: (02) 9519 3679
www.icedaffair.com.au
Supplier of sugarcraft equipment

About the author

Well known and highly respected in the sugarcraft industry, Lindy Smith has over 20 years' experience in sugarcrafting. Lindy is a designer who likes to share her love of sugarcraft and inspire fellow enthusiasts by writing books and teaching. Lindy is the author of 13 cake decorating titles for D&C, the most recent including: *The Contemporary Cake Decorating Bible, Bake Me I'm Yours... Cupcake Celebration, Bake Me I'm Yours... Cookie, Cakes to Inspire and Desire* and *Party Animal Cakes.*

Lindy's teaching takes her all around the world, giving her the opportunity to educate and inspire, while also learning about local traditions and cake decorating issues. This knowledge is ultimately then fed back into her work. She has appeared on television many times and presented a sugarcraft series on *Good Food Live.*

Lindy also heads Lindy's Cakes Ltd, a well-established business that runs her online shop, www.lindyscakes.co.uk, and her cake decorating workshops both in the UK and abroad. In 2012, Lindy won *Insight Magazine*'s Business Woman of the Year. Katherine Benson, the magazine editor, said: "Lindy Smith is a remarkable woman. Not only does she boast high-level skills to create her own designs, but she thrives on helping others achieve their goals when it comes to making that cake not only taste good but look good too. Her range of knowledge is extensive and from her website to her books, cutters and stencils and classes, Lindy has shown that being business savvy isn't all about profiting yourself, but also about profiting others too.

To see what Lindy is currently doing, become a fan of Lindy's Cakes on Facebook or follow Lindy on Twitter. For baking advice and a wealth of information, visit her blog via the Lindy's Cakes website: **www.lindyscakes.co.uk**

Acknowledgments

A big thank you goes to Daisy, one of my uni students, who spent a summer perfecting her colour mixing and sugar modelling skills to bring you the colour wheel and other colour examples in the introductory section of this book. You never know Daisy, maybe your natural flair for colours and a chemistry degree will lead you down an exciting career path!!

As always I'd like to thank my team; although not directly involved, they allow me the space and time to create. Thank you also for all your varied and helpful comments and opinions. I'm always interested in what you all think, as you are a very good barometer of opinion.

A big thank you goes to Squires Kitchen, who kindly supplied their wonderful range of paste and dust colours for use in the Index of Paste Colours and the cakes throughout this book. Thank you also to Sandra from Panache Interiors (**www.panache-interiors.com**) for letting me dive into her wonderful fabric boxes and choose as much beautiful luxurious material as I liked for the mood boards and styled photos – what a delight!

I would like to thank David & Charles, my publishers, for giving this book the budget to go 'on location'. I have wanted to do this for such a long time; it makes such a difference to the end result, as the cakes can 'breathe' and be themselves in a natural setting – stunning. A final thank you to my amazing photographer, Jack from Bang Wallop; Jack, it was a delight working with you, the step photography is clear and vibrant and the finished cakes look simply fabulous.

index

A DAVID & CHARLES BOOK
© F&W Media International, Ltd 2013

David & Charles is an imprint of F&W Media International, Ltd
Brunel House, Forde Close, Newton Abbot, TQ12 4PU, UK

F&W Media International, Ltd is a subsidiary of F+W Media, Inc
10151 Carver Road, Cincinnati OH45242, USA

Text and Designs © Lindy Smith 2013
Layout and Photography © F&W Media International, Ltd 2013
except: pages 16, 18, 26, 28, 36, 38, 50, 60, 70, 72, 82, 92, 94, 104, 116:
colour inspiration photographs © Lindy Smith

Page 48: 'Teacups' card by Phoenix Trading © Tina Schneider
Page 58: Chrysotomontum © Rex Ray, 2005 **www.rexray.com**
Page 102: Unique Graphics ring binder ©
Staples **www.staples.co.uk**
Page 114: Necklace © Ladies Who Lunch Couture Jewellery
www.ladieswholunchjewellery.com

First published in the UK and USA in 2013

Names of manufacturers and product ranges
are provided for the information of readers, with
no intention to infringe copyright or trademarks.

A catalogue record for this book is available
from the British Library.

ISBN-13: 978-1-4463-0237-8 hardback
ISBN-10: 1-4463-0237-7 hardback

ISBN-13: 978-1-4463-0238-5 paperback
ISBN-10: 1-4463-0238-5 paperback

Printed in China by RR Donnelley for:
F&W Media International, Ltd
Brunel House, Forde Close, Newton
Abbot, TQ12 4PU, UK

10 9 8 7 6 5 4 3 2 1

Publisher: Alison Myer
Craft Business Manager: Ame Verso
Multi-Channel Content Editor: James Brooks
Project Editor: Jo Richardson
Art Editor: Sarah Underhill
Photographer: All photography by
Jack Kirby except Eastern Infusion
(page 80) by Victoria Blackie
Cover Photographer: Mark Scott
Senior Production Controller: Kelly Smith

F+W Media publishes high quality books on
a wide range of subjects.
For more great book ideas visit: **www.
stitchcraftcreate.co.uk**

Claim your **FREE** craft eBook from Stitch Craft Create!

Download a fabulous FREE eBook from our handpicked selection at:
www.stitchcraftcreate.co.uk/ideas

Then visit our bookstore to buy more great books like these…

THE CONTEMPORARY CAKE DECORATING BIBLE
Lindy Smith

ISBN-13: 978-0-7153-3836-0

Discover everything you need to know to create celebration cakes that are beautiful, unique and truly contemporary! Features over 150 techniques and more than 80 projects, including tiered cakes, wonky cakes, mini cakes, cupcakes and cookies.

CHIC & UNIQUE VINTAGE CAKES
Zoe Clark

ISBN-13: 978-1-4463-0284-2

10 incredible cake designs accompanied by two smaller designs for vintage-inspired cupcakes, cookies, fondant fancies and more. Learn how to make elegant tiered cakes and amazing gravity-defying novelty cakes, including sewing machines and vintage dress stands.

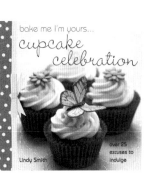

BAKE ME I'M YOURS… CUPCAKE CELEBRATION
Lindy Smith

ISBN-13: 978-0-7153-3770-7

Celebrate in style, with over 25 irresistible cupcake ideas from bestselling author Lindy Smith. Add that special touch to every occasion following the beautiful designs and delicious recipes.

CAKE CRAFT MADE EASY
Fiona Pearce

ISBN-13: 978-1-4463-0291-0

Essential cake decorating techniques explained, from simple buttercream piping through to stenciling with royal icing, making sugar flowers, and decorating novelty cakes. With 16 cake designs, plus 12 free video demonstrations online.

www.stitchcraftcreate.co.uk/books

All details correct at time of printing.